WordPress for Education

Create interactive and engaging e-learning websites
with WordPress

Adam D. Scott

PUBLISHING

BIRMINGHAM - MUMBAI

WordPress for Education

First published: June 2012

Production Reference: 1010612

Published by Packt Publishing Ltd.
Livery Place
35 Livery Street
Birmingham B3 2PB, UK.

ISBN 978-1-84951-820-8

www.packtpub.com

Cover Image by Asher Wishkerman (a.wishkerman@mpic.de)

Credits

Author
Adam D. Scott

Reviewers
John Eckman

Sam Rose

Acquisition Editor
Sarah Cullington

Lead Technical Editor
Sonali Tharwani

Technical Editor
Felix Vijay

Project Coordinator
Leena Purkait

Proofreader
Lisa Brady

Indexer
Rekha Nair

Production Coordinator
Alwin Roy

Cover Work
Alwin Roy

About the Author

Adam D. Scott is an educator, designer, digital book developer, husband, and father living in Connecticut. He has been a classroom teacher for six years where he focuses on web technologies with project-based outcomes. He writes about the intersection of design, technology, and learning on his personal site, www.adamdscott.com.

I would like to thank my wife, Abigail, for lovingly supporting all my ideas, no matter how far-fetched; my sons, Riley and Harrison, who are a constant source of energy and inspiration; my parents for encouraging my interests in technology and learning; Judy, for giving me the opportunity and freedom to explore the world of education; Sarah and Sonali, for their encouragement and editorial guidance; Leena, for her management and organizational assistance; John and Sam, for their expertise and thoughtful advice; and the WordPress core team and plugin developers, for creating an incredible platform.

About the Reviewers

John Eckman is a digital strategist and consultant, and one of the founding organizers of WordCamp Boston. He has created and maintained a number of popular WordPress plugins, and is active in multiple open source communities and projects.

He blogs at www.openparenthesis.org, tweets as @jeckman, and speaks frequently at conferences on open source content management, e-commerce, and community. He holds a PhD from the University of Washington, Seattle, an MIS from Northeastern University, Boston, and a BA from Boston University.

He has technically reviewed the following books for *Packt Publishing*:

- *WordPress 3 Ultimate Security*
- *WordPress 3 for Business Bloggers*
- *WordPress 3 Cookbook*

> I'd like to thank Packt Publishing and the WordPress community (developers, designers, and users), without whom none of this would be possible.

Sam Rose is a student and will be a Computer Science graduate soon. He has carried out book reviews for a variety of technologies and subjects including Ruby, Rails, ANTLR, WordPress, and Career Development.

He enjoys working with Ruby and Python most, as well as dabbling in newer languages on the side such as Scala and Haskell.

When not coding, he can be found blogging at http://samwho.co.uk.

www.PacktPub.com

Support files, eBooks, discount offers, and more

You might want to visit www.PacktPub.com for support files and downloads related to your book.

Did you know that Packt offers eBook versions of every book published, with PDF and ePub files available? You can upgrade to the eBook version at www.PacktPub.com and as a print book customer, you are entitled to a discount on the eBook copy. Get in touch with us at service@packtpub.com for more details.

At www.PacktPub.com, you can also read a collection of free technical articles, sign up for a range of free newsletters and receive exclusive discounts and offers on Packt books and eBooks.

http://PacktLib.PacktPub.com

Do you need instant solutions to your IT questions? PacktLib is Packt's online digital book library. Here, you can access, read and search across Packt's entire library of books.

Why Subscribe?

- Fully searchable across every book published by Packt
- Copy and paste, print, and bookmark content
- On demand and accessible via web browser

Free Access for Packt account holders

If you have an account with Packt at www.PacktPub.com, you can use this to access PacktLib today and view nine entirely free books. Simply use your login credentials for immediate access.

Table of Contents

Preface

In the summer of 2008, I began a personal blog powered by WordPress and quickly fell for the ease and extensibility of the platform. As an educator, I had tried a number of tools to power course websites, but had to be satisfied with the results. With the fall semester approaching, I decided to try WordPress in the classroom. As the academic year progressed, I found that I was able to effectively mold WordPress to fit the needs of my students.

In recent years the popularity of WordPress has exploded. It is estimated that nearly 15 percent of the top million websites and 22 percent of all new websites are powered by WordPress (http://wordpress.org/news/2011/08/state-of-the-word/). These staggering numbers can be attributed to the WordPress community, which has built thousands of useful plugins atop of the already impressive WordPress core. As an increasing number of educators use WordPress in the classroom, the education-specific plugin library grows, making WordPress an ideal solution for educators.

What this book covers

Chapter 1, Installing and Configuring WordPress, covers the installation of WordPress on a web server, explores the WordPress dashboard, and discusses the difference between posts and pages.

Chapter 2, Setting Up Our Class Site, covers how to build a basic course website by adding and editing posts and pages, changing the look of the site with themes, and enhancing the site's functionality with widgets.

Chapter 3, Enhancing WordPress with Plugins, discusses the use of WordPress plugins to add additional features to our site. This chapter will guide you through the process of installing plugins and provide a list of plugins that are useful in an education setting.

Chapter 4, Enabling a Multisite Network, describes the process of running a network of sites from a single WordPress installation. This is ideal for powering student blogs and portfolios.

Chapter 5, Creating a Social Network with BuddyPress, covers how the BuddyPress plugin can be used to turn WordPress into a socially collaborative environment.

Chapter 6, BuddyPress Courseware, covers how the ScholarPress BuddyPress Courseware plugin can be used to turn WordPress into a fully-functioning course management system with course content, assignments, bibliographies, and course calendar.

Chapter 7, Site Management, discusses how to keep WordPress up to date, secure our WordPress installation, and ensure that the WordPress database is backed up.

Self-hosted WordPress or WordPress.com

In this book, we will be discussing the self-hosted WordPress platform. WordPress.com is a commercial web site, powered by WordPress, that allows users to easily sign up for a free blog site. While WordPress.com is great for dipping our toes into the world of WordPress, it does not offer the rich features and extensibility of a self-hosted WordPress installation. For the same reason, this book focuses on the self-hosted WordPress platform, available at WordPress.org.

Who this book is for

WordPress for Education is for classroom educators at the K-12 and college level who are interested in powering a course website or managing a network of student blogs with WordPress. Throughout the book, I do not assume prior knowledge of WordPress or experience with blogging software. This book aims to simplify seemingly daunting technical tasks such as installing the software on a web server or managing backups. The book is also useful for institution or district-level IT professionals who are interested in deploying WordPress. This book acts as a practical and easy-to-understand guide to WordPress in the classroom, aiming to increase online communication between instructors and students.

What you need for this book

The only requirements for this book are a web connected computer, a web browser, and a self-hosted WordPress installation. Other tools that may be of use are a text editor and FTP software. In subsequent chapters, we will recommend appropriate open source options to fill these needs.

Conventions

In this book, you will find a number of styles of text that distinguish between different kinds of information. Here are some examples of these styles, and an explanation of their meaning.

Code words in text are shown as follows: "If the new site was to be www.example.org/student1, simply enter student 1."

A block of code is set as follows:

```
// ** MySQL settings - You can get this info from your web host **
/** The name of the database for WordPress */
define('DB_NAME', 'putyourdbnamehere');
/** MySQL database username */
define('DB_USER', 'usernamehere');
/** MySQL database password */
```

When we wish to draw your attention to a particular part of a code block, the relevant lines or items are set in bold:

```
// ** MySQL settings - You can get this info from your web host **
/** The name of the database for WordPress */
define('DB_NAME', 'putyourdbnamehere');
/** MySQL database username */
define('DB_USER', 'usernamehere');
/** MySQL database password */
```

New terms and **important words** are shown in bold. Words that you see on the screen, in menus or dialog boxes for example, appear in the text like this: "Click on the **OK** button."

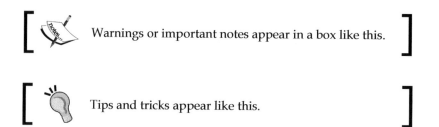

Warnings or important notes appear in a box like this.

Tips and tricks appear like this.

Reader feedback

Feedback from our readers is always welcome. Let us know what you think about this book—what you liked or may have disliked. Reader feedback is important for us to develop titles that you really get the most out of.

To send us general feedback, simply send an e-mail to feedback@packtpub.com, and mention the book title via the subject of your message.

If there is a book that you need and would like to see us publish, please send us a note in the **SUGGEST A TITLE** form on www.packtpub.com or e-mail suggest@packtpub.com.

If there is a topic that you have expertise in and you are interested in either writing or contributing to a book, see our author guide on www.packtpub.com/authors.

Customer support

Now that you are the proud owner of a Packt book, we have a number of things to help you to get the most from your purchase.

Errata

Although we have taken every care to ensure the accuracy of our content, mistakes do happen. If you find a mistake in one of our books—maybe a mistake in the text or the code—we would be grateful if you would report this to us. By doing so, you can save other readers from frustration and help us improve subsequent versions of this book. If you find any errata, please report them by visiting http://www.packtpub.com/support, selecting your book, clicking on the **errata submission form** link, and entering the details of your errata. Once your errata are verified, your submission will be accepted and the errata will be uploaded on our website, or added to any list of existing errata, under the Errata section of that title. Any existing errata can be viewed by selecting your title from http://www.packtpub.com/support.

Piracy

Piracy of copyright material on the Internet is an ongoing problem across all media. At Packt, we take the protection of our copyright and licenses very seriously. If you come across any illegal copies of our works, in any form, on the Internet, please provide us with the location address or website name immediately so that we can pursue a remedy.

Please contact us at `copyright@packtpub.com` with a link to the suspected pirated material.

We appreciate your help in protecting our authors, and our ability to bring you valuable content.

Questions

You can contact us at `questions@packtpub.com` if you are having a problem with any aspect of the book, and we will do our best to address it.

1
Installing and Configuring WordPress

Running our own hosted WordPress installation will provide us with power and flexibility that is not available through free blog services. In this chapter, we'll walk through the process of installing WordPress on a server. Once WordPress is installed we'll explore the WordPress dashboard interface, learn the difference between **posts** and **pages**, and adjust our site's settings.

Installing WordPress

To power our site, we will need access to a web server. This can be achieved by either purchasing a web hosting account or discussing web hosting possibilities with the IT department within our institution.

As of version 3.2 or later, the requirements for WordPress are PHP 5.2.4 or greater and MySQL 5.0 or greater. If these acronyms seem frightening, don't worry, just be aware that PHP is the web scripting language that will power our WordPress installation and MySQL is the database that will store all of our content.

Many educational institutions have begun to offer WordPress installations to faculty, staff, and students. These installations come free-of-charge with a domain name already in place. Speak with your IT department to see if your school provides this service.

If your institution does not provide WordPress installations, we will cover two additional ways in which WordPress can be installed. If you plan to purchase web hosting from a third-party company, follow the instructions in the purchased hosting portion of the chapter. If your institution or IT department provides web hosting services, but does not provide WordPress installations, follow the instructions for manually installing WordPress.

Purchased hosting

Installing WordPress is a relatively straightforward procedure. In fact, the WordPress team has dubbed it the *Famous 5-Minute Install*. It can, however, require a bit of technical know-how. For that reason, I recommend using a web hosting service that offers a "one-click" WordPress installation. Essentially, this means that the service will run the installation for us.

Choosing a web host can feel a bit overwhelming. Luckily, WordPress offers a list of recommended web hosts (`http://wordpress.org/hosting/`). Each of these hosts, with the exception of **Laughing Squid**, offers "one-click" installations of WordPress and due to their wide use among the WordPress community, it is often easy to find solutions to any hosting related technical problem. While these are the hosts recommended by WordPress, nearly any modern commercial web host will meet the WordPress requirements. If you are interested in performing a manual WordPress installation, follow the instructions given in the in-house hosting portion of the chapter.

The hosts recommended by WordPress are:

- Bluehost—`http://bluehost.com`
- DreamHost—`http://dreamhost.com`
- MediaTemple—`http://mediatemple.net/wordpress-webhosting.php`
- Laughing Squid—`http://laughingsquid.us`

Once we have selected a web host, the next step is to choose an appropriate hosting plan. For a simple class site, the basic plan of nearly any web host will work well. For sites that utilize the WordPress MultiSite or BuddyPress features discussed later in the book, we may need to choose something more robust. These sites tend to use more bandwidth and require a larger database, making a more fully-featured hosting plan a wise decision. If you are unsure of which plan will work best for your site, contact the hosting provider and they will guide you to the service that is best suited for your needs.

I have had a very positive experience working with Media Temple's Grid-Service hosting. At $20 per month, it is the most expensive hosting option listed, but I am currently using a single account to power several WordPress installations, including a BuddyPress site.

Installing WordPress with purchased hosting

The first step in setting up our hosting is obtaining a domain name. Domain names are the public address of your site and must be purchased and renewed annually. The cost of domain registration varies but is most often around $10-$15 per year.

To register our domain, we must find an available domain name. A domain name is a unique identifier such as example.org. Domain names end with top-level domain names such as .com, .net, .org, or .info. For educational use, I recommend avoiding .com as it is designed for commercial services and as the most commonly used domain extension, it is also the most difficult to find available domain names.

> **Example URLs**
> Throughout this book I will use example.org as our sample URL. Anywhere you see example.org, it should be replaced with your unique URL.

Once we have found a suitable domain name, we can continue setting up an account with our chosen hosting provider. With our hosting account activated, we are ready to install WordPress. MediaTemple offers its customers a service entitled *1-Click Applications*, which will install a WordPress site. Each hosting company listed will have their own unique interface and clear documentation for this service, but look for choices such as *1-Click Applications* or *Simple Scripts*.

At this point of the installation we will be asked to name the database and provide a database table prefix. By default these are wp, but for security reasons it is recommended that the user should change the name to something unique. For the sample site, we will use something more descriptive to name the database and database prefix. Using descriptive names will prevent future confusion should we install more WordPress sites at a later date.

- **Database name: wpcourse**
- **Database prefix: course_** (note that the database prefix is followed by an underscore)

Finishing the installation

To complete the installation, we will visit the WordPress **Welcome** page. To access this page, type `http://example.org/wp-admin/install.php` in your browser (remember to replace `example.org` with the name of your site).

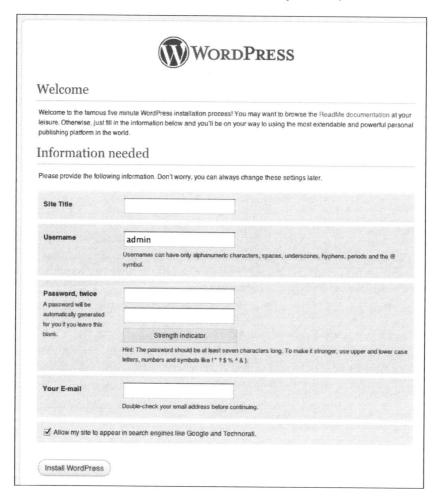

From the **Welcome** page, we are able to enter the title of our site, create a username and password, enter our e-mail address, and choose if we would like our site to be available to search engines such as Google and Bing.

Choosing a username

By default WordPress selects `admin` as the username. For security reasons, it is advisable to choose a unique name.

Once the information has been entered, click on the **Install WordPress** button to complete the installation process. We will then receive a success message and be given the option to log in to WordPress. WordPress is now installed and our site is live!

Manually installing WordPress

Some educators may be lucky enough to have access to institution running web hosting accounts. Speak with your IT department about this possibility and ensure that the servers meet the PHP and MySQL requirements needed to run WordPress. In this scenario, we may need to perform a manual installation of WordPress.

Before performing a manual WordPress installation, we will need two crucial pieces of software: an FTP program and a text editor.

FTP (File Transfer Protocol) programs allow us to transfer files from our computer to a web server. FileZilla (`http://filezilla-project.org`) is an open source FTP program that is available cross platform (Windows, Mac OS X, and Linux).

Text editors allow us to edit text files in a range of formats. When installing WordPress manually, we will use our text editor to make changes to the WordPress PHP files. If you do not already have a specialized text editor, both Windows and Mac OS X come pre-equipped with basic text editors (Notepad for Windows, Text Edit for Mac OS X, and Nano or gedit for Linux).

With our FTP program and text editor, we are ready to complete the *Famous 5-minute install* process.

1. Download WordPress: Visit `WordPress.org`, available through download, and unzip the latest version of the WordPress software.

2. Create a database: The most common means for creating a database is to use the tool **phpMyAdmin**. This is a web page that allows us to administer our MySQL databases. If phpMyAdmin is not already available, documentation and a download link are available through `http://phpmyadmin.net`.

Institutionally managed accounts may not permit users to install phpMyAdmin, but may provide other means for creating databases. Speak with your IT administrators to gain a clear understanding of your institution's policies.

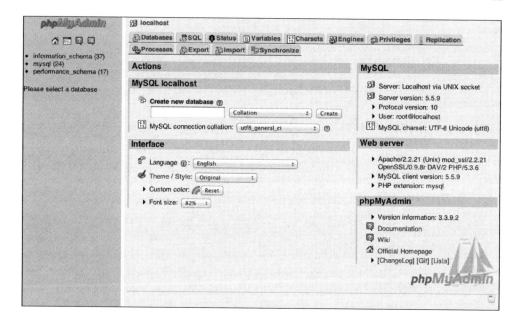

- Within phpMyAdmin, create a database by clicking on the **Databases** tab, naming the database in the **Create new database** textbox and clicking on the **Create** button. In this example, I've called the database **wpcourse**.

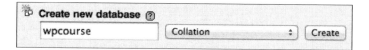

- Be sure to note the following information about your database:

    - The **Database name** is the name you have given the new database.

    - The **Database username** is the username you use to log in to the database.

    - The **Database password** is the password you use to log in to the database.

    - The **Database host** is the name given by the host. This is typically localhost.

Of these, only the database name is generated by us. The remaining information should be supplied by the IT department or hosting provider.

In this example installation, my database information is as follows:

- **Database name**: wpcourse
- **Database username**: administrator
- **Database password**: xyz123
- **Database host**: localhost

> **The database host**
>
> The majority of hosting companies use localhost as the database hostname, but it may vary depending on provider. The WordPress Codex provides a list of database hostnames for a number of popular hosting companies (http://codex.wordpress.org/Editing_wp-config. php). If you are working with the IT department at your institution, speak with them regarding the database host information.

3. Create a copy of the `wp-config-sample.php` and rename the file `wp-config-sample-copy.php`. This ensures that there is a backup of the initial `wp-config` file.

4. Rename the `wp-config-sample.php` file to `wp-config.php`. This file is located in the main directory of the downloaded `WordPress` folder.

5. Fill in your database details in the `wp-config.php` file. To do this, open `wp-config.php` with your text editor and locate the following:

```
// ** MySQL settings - You can get this info from your web host **
//
/** The name of the database for WordPress */
define('DB_NAME', 'putyourdbnamehere');
/** MySQL database username */
define('DB_USER', 'usernamehere');
/** MySQL database password */
define('DB_PASSWORD', 'yourpasswordhere');
/** MySQL hostname */
define('DB_HOST', 'localhost');
```

To edit the file:

- Replace `putyourdbnamehere` with your database name. In our example, this is **wpcourse**.

- Replace `usernamehere` with your database username. In our example, this is **administrator**.

- ° Replace `yourpasswordhere` with your database password. In our example, this is **xyz123**.
- ° If necessary, replace **localhost** with your MySQL hostname.

This information will now be changed to look something like this (be sure to use your own database information):

```
// ** MySQL settings - You can get this info from your web host **
//
/** The name of the database for WordPress */
define('DB_NAME', wpcourse);
/** MySQL database username */
define('DB_USER', 'administrator');
/** MySQL database password */
define('DB_PASSWORD', 'xyz123');
/** MySQL hostname */
define('DB_HOST', 'localhost');
```

6. Update the WordPress security keys within the `wp-config.php` file. The security keys are a long, random collection of characters used to encrypt user information. To create the security keys visit `https://api.wordpress.org/secret-key/1.1/salt/`.

This will create a set of random keys such as:

```
define('AUTH_KEY',          'mJZ!HZUYS^EGrg~I5xJLCdnQ|xq?%56c;~@
17g5)Eb2n+I/zrv<cqBdFtjA^jp%/');
define('SECURE_AUTH_KEY',   'NH#,QsmxIV lig~~{;|~T<i-x+_(`En>+Z?;@
H+tg%/w/AbNb||u9?HB>I*W8]>0');
define('LOGGED_IN_KEY',     'CfC-VBrKNXYiR9d.V&Wj=IJ/P)_3fNgBq(-
u9HW 2kD[KpX,.$n&K}|kvVa{}+1');
define('NONCE_KEY',         '%Vo8&Fq+fy78f4mJE`QoXcrW<Qw:|TvDu<f~Dt
l]$Hr|h@:1,sC{CmJ/z,ZMv1g(');
define('AUTH_SALT',         '`+>ED885rL]r4TLU.P77m23.x$=<-@--
<JEC>aKd0{{bM5VIc54]g*b6T[c>aUVM');
define('SECURE_AUTH_SALT',  'm^{}c[1Fx/FT!3<5OP+_H^E0+p.W<rV|ADSxT
=DMHkTaPnrdxY6R!bJbrzSoeJM');
define('LOGGED_IN_SALT',    'WapX3 yi;iG<x-&T)}qEAF18_J#<%wSHjMS*6c
WTp=I:WWb|N|}L_84KE4>muI6N');
define('NONCE_SALT',        '?a2b|4pawNj4.4YX;n9LZGxXW/|?zd@
JJ(|AlO*@VdUna-*[$VQQ*6-_MF{olRcP');
```

Add the security key to the `wp-config.php` file by copying it and replacing the default keys contained within the file.

7. **Upload WordPress to the server.** Using the credentials supplied by your IT department/web host, access your server through the FTP software and drag the entire contents of the WordPress directory to your server.

8. Run the installation. Run the WordPress installation script by going to `http://example.org/wp-admin/install.php` in your browser and filling in the appropriate information.

This covers the basic installation of WordPress. The WordPress Codex has a variety of instructions covering a range of hosting options and can serve as an excellent resource (`http://codex.wordpress.org/Installing_WordPress`).

WordPress overview

To log in to our WordPress site, visit `www.example.org/wp-login.php`. I would recommend creating a browser bookmark for the login page, as it will be the gateway to your WordPress site.

Once we have entered the credentials created during the installation process, we will be taken to the **Dashboard** of the WordPress interface.

At the top of the **Dashboard** is the WordPress Toolbar. The admin bar will remain at the top of our browser window throughout the WordPress interface, allowing us to quickly visit our public website, check for updates, administer comments, add/edit posts and pages, and log out of WordPress.

On the left hand side of the Toolbar we see the WordPress logo followed by the name of our site. The name of the site is a link that, when clicked, will take us to our site's public home page. This is a quick and easy way to view our site.

At the right side of the Toolbar we will see our username. Hovering over our username presents us with the option to **Log Out** of WordPress. Below the username are the **Screen Options** and **Help** links. **Screen Options** allows us to manage the appearance of the current WordPress screen. The **Help** link opens a unique help guide for each section of the site.

The left sidebar offers links to all of the different tasks we can perform within WordPress, allowing us to manage the posts, pages, settings, look, and functionality of our site.

The large, center column of the dashboard is designed to provide an overview of our site. The first time we access the WordPress dashboard, the center column will contain a large **Welcome to your new WordPress** site section, designed to provide an overview of WordPress and its functionality.

The **Right Now** area offers an overview of what is happening on the site by listing the number of posts, pages, categories, tags, comments, and comment details. It also displays which version of WordPress we are currently running.

Through the **QuickPress** option, the dashboard offers us a quick way to write a post without the need to leave the dashboard.

Within the center column of the dashboard we can also see the latest WordPress news, a list of recent popular plugins, recent site comments, and a list of recent links to our site.

Creating posts and pages

The two essential functions of WordPress are its ability to quickly and easily create posts and pages. Posts are the primary content of a typical WordPress blog site. They are individual chunks of content, similar to news items, which are used to post frequent and timely updates to the site. Blog posts tend to be read in reverse chronological order on the site or by subscribers in feed readers. Pages make up the individual web pages of our site. Pages tend to be less frequently updated and are typically accessed through menus. For instance, we may have a page on our site that contains the course syllabus. When we make a change to that syllabus, we can write a new post alerting our students of the change.

Writing a new post

Posts are one of the foundations of WordPress. Posts can otherwise be thought of as blog posts, updates, or news. In terms of our class, posts are a great way to publish assignments, due date reminders, supplemental course content, and any news we may deem relevant to the course. Posts can be tagged and organized so that they may be sorted or searched by subject matter or keywords. Students may even use an RSS reader to subscribe to your posts so that they will never miss an update.

To write a new post, hover over **Posts** in the left sidebar of the WordPress dashboard and choose the **Add New** option.

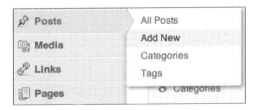

This presents us with the **New Post** screen. From this screen we are able to write and publish posts. Creating a post is as simple as typing in the large input area and pressing the **Publish** button. Give your post a brief descriptive title by typing in the **Enter title here** input area.

The larger text area below the title bar is where we will type the post. It works much like a Word processor, allowing us to type content as well as edit the formatting of our text.

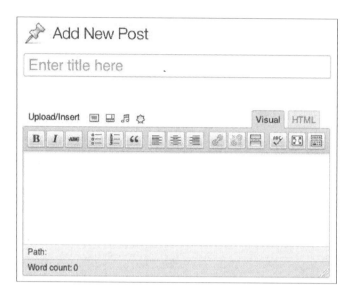

Once we have finished writing our post, we can publish it to our site by clicking on the blue **Publish** button located on the right-hand area of the screen. A **view post** link will appear within a yellow box above the page title, allowing us to quickly view the new post on our site.

Creating a page

Creating a new page works similar to writing a post in WordPress. From anywhere within the WordPress dashboard, click on the arrow next to **Pages** in the left sidebar and choose **Add New**. Enter a title for the new page in the top text area. The large text area below is used to create the body of our page. To publish the page, click on the blue **Publish** button located on the right hand side of the screen.

As an example, we may wish to create an **About** page to describe the purpose of our site. Enter **About** into the top text area and type a brief description of the site within the body text area. Once the description is complete, click on the **Publish** button to create the page.

Once the page is published, click on the **view page** link that appears within the yellow box above the page title, to see the post live on our site.

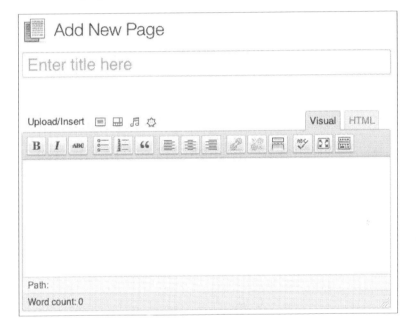

Settings

While WordPress works great right out of the box, adjusting a few of our site's settings can improve both our experience as WordPress users as well as the experience of our students and site users. To view the settings categories, click on the drop-down arrow next to **Settings** at the bottom of the left sidebar.

General Settings

General Settings allows us to edit the basic settings of our site. Here we can update the site title, site tagline, site address, administrator e-mail, as well as date and time information. One of the first changes I make to a fresh WordPress installation is to update the time zone to correctly reflect my location.

Another important **General Setting** to update is the tagline. Our site's tagline appears below the site title in most WordPress themes. By default the tagline reads, *Just another WordPress* site. Within the **General Settings** we are able to change the tagline to reflect a better description of our site.

Writing Settings

Writing Settings gives us greater control as to how we input content into WordPress. Within these settings, we are able to control the textbox formatting, change the default categories of posts and links, add the **Press This** bookmarklet, and enable posting via e-mail and desktop applications.

I would recommend adding the **Press This** bookmarklet to your browser. A bookmarklet is a small piece of JavaScript code that, when installed as a browser bookmark, allows you to interact with any web page. To install the **Press This** bookmarklet, click-and-drag the **Press This** button to your browser's bookmark bar. With this bookmarklet, you are now able to quickly create a post from anywhere on the web. For example, if you encounter a great class resource while browsing, click on the **Press This** bookmarklet and quickly add a post to inform your students. This post will automatically title itself with the title of the website you are visiting and add a link to the page.

The following screenshot shows you the **Press This** bookmarklet in action:

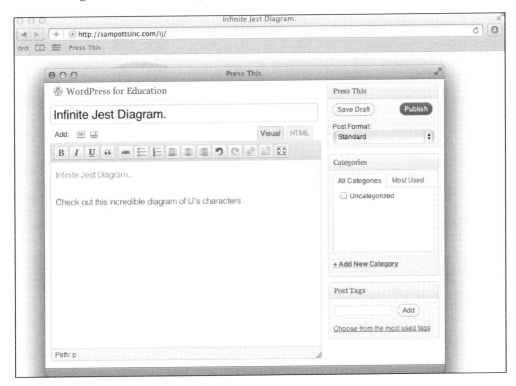

Reading Settings

Reading Settings allows us to make changes to the way our students or readers interact with our content both on the site itself and within the site's RSS feed. Within **Reading Settings**, we can adjust the home page of our site, the number of posts that appear on single page, and the type of RSS feed that will be available.

What is RSS?

RSS stands for Real Simple Syndication and allows readers to easily subscribe to a site using a feed reader such as Google Reader (http://google.com/reader). New posts will automatically appear in the feed reader, saving the site user the trouble of checking for site updates.

Discussion Settings

WordPress enables site visitors to leave comments. Our site's **Discussion Settings** refers to the comments left on our site's posts and pages. We can make adjustments to our site's discussion settings to suit our preferences or even disable comments altogether. For example, un-checking the **Allow people to post comments on new articles** box will disable comments.

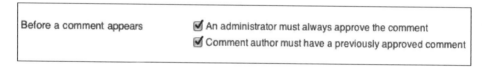

If you choose to allow comments, I would suggest checking the **An administrator must always approve the comment** checkbox. This will prevent any inappropriate or off-topic comments from appearing on our site.

Media Settings

Media Settings allows us to control the size and location of the images and videos used in our site.

Privacy Settings

When installing WordPress we were able to choose if we would like search engines to index our site. Within the privacy settings we can adjust this setting if we choose to reverse our initial decision.

Permalinks

By default, WordPress creates URLs for our posts that use the post ID along with question marks and numbers. These default URLs wind up looking something like: `http://example.org/?p=123`. By changing the **Permalink Settings** we can adjust our post URLs to be more memorable (not to mention much more aesthetically pleasing), such as: `http://example.org/2012/12/post-name/`.

WordPress provides several choices to easily change our permalink structure to one of the most common settings, but we can create our own structure using special tags provided by WordPress.

Chart of permalink tags	
%year%	Numerical year of the post
%monthnum%	Numerical month of the post
%day%	Numerical day of the month
%hour%	Numerical hour of the day
%minute%	Numerical minute of the hour
%second%	Numerical second of the minute
%post_id%	The unique numerical ID of the post
%postname%	The name of your post
%category%	The category of your post
%tag%	The tags used in your post
%author%	The name of the post author

If we wanted to create a custom permalink structure for our site that displayed the year, post category, and post name we would enter the following into the **Custom Structure** text area:

```
/%year%/%category%/%postname%/
```

Now, a post written in October of 2012, titled `Essay`, and given the category of `assignments` would appear as such:

```
http://example.org/2012/assignments/Essay/
```

Summary

In this chapter we've covered everything we need to get started with WordPress. We've chosen a web host, installed WordPress, explored the WordPress dashboard, learned the difference between posts and pages, and configured WordPress by updating our site's settings. In the next chapter we'll look at how WordPress posts and pages can be used to build a course website.

2
Setting Up Our Class Site

Now that WordPress is installed and we have explored the basics of the WordPress interface, it is time to set up our class site. The class site will serve as an example throughout the book, displaying how WordPress can be utilized as a means for instructors to communicate with their students. In this chapter we'll cover how to add and edit the pages and posts needed for a typical class site. We'll also enhance the look of our site with themes, add additional functionality using widgets, and improve our site's navigation with a custom menu.

Basics of post and page editing

While they perform two different functions, the post and page editors look and act in a very similar way. As described in *Chapter 1, Installing and Configuring WordPress*, creating a new post or page is as simple as choosing the **Add New** option, typing some text, and clicking on the **Publish** button. Fortunately, WordPress provides a great deal of flexibility when it comes to the content and formatting of a post or page.

When writing or editing posts/pages, we are given the choice of using either the **Visual** editor or HTML editor. By default we are presented with the **Visual** editor, which acts similarly to a word processor. Clicking on the **HTML** tab will switch to the **HTML** editor, allowing those who know HTML the ability to directly edit the markup of a post or page.

When in **Visual** editor mode, there is a row of buttons between the **Title** and **Post Editing** area that allow us to control the formatting of our text. The first several buttons perform basic text formatting such as applying a bold typeface, italics, strikethroughs, ordered lists, unordered lists, block quotes, and text alignment.

Hyperlinks are the foundation of the web and an easy way to point students to resources, external readings, and multimedia content. The **Insert/Edit Link** button allows us to turn text into hyperlinks while the **Unlink** button easily removes them.

The **Insert More Tag** button allows us to create breaking points for our posts. Any text or media before the more tag will appear on our site's post page. A student or site visitor will need to click on the **continue reading** link to finish reading the remainder of the post. This is helpful when a post is longer than usual, as it will prevent a single post's contents from commanding the majority of the page.

WordPress also includes a spellcheck feature in a variety of languages and a **Full Screen Mode** that will remove the distractions of the page and provide us with a larger area of input. These are helpful if you choose to do your post or page writing from within the WordPress interface.

Previewing and publishing options

Clicking on the blue **Publish** button will instantly publish our posts and pages to our site. Within the **Publish** box we are presented with a variety of publishing options.

Perhaps the most useful option is the **Preview** button. When we click on the **Preview** button, WordPress will present us with a preview of our post or page as it will appear on our site. Once we have viewed the preview, we are able to continue editing or publish our content.

The **Save Draft** button will save our post or page, with a status of **Draft**, so that we may return at a later time to complete it. The **Status** area allows us to see if our post or page is currently in draft or has already been published.

By editing the **Visibility** of a post or page, we can choose if it is public, password protected, or private. Public is the default for all posts and pages. Using Password protecting pages can be useful when we wish to only share information with a specific class or group without making it public.

To password protect a page or post:

1. Click on the **Edit** link next to **Visibility**.
2. Select the **Password Protected** option.
3. Enter a password.
4. Click on the **OK** button.

Posts and pages set to **Private** will only be available to you or other registered site users.

New posts and pages are automatically published as soon as we click on the **Publish** button. However, we can schedule these for future dates and times. This can be incredibly useful when dealing with time-sensitive information. For example, this could be used to publish assignments that students should not have access to in advance, without requiring the author to be online at the time when the post goes live.

To schedule a post or page to publish:

1. Click on the **Edit** link next to **Publish immediately**.
2. Choose the **publish date and time** option.
3. Click on the **OK** button.
4. Click on the blue **Schedule** button, which has replaced the **Publish** button.

From within the **Publish** box we are also given the option of deleting the draft of a page or post. To delete a draft, click on the red **Move to Trash** link.

Pages

Adding a selection of **Pages** can turn our WordPress site from a simple blog, to a fully-functioning course site. In this section, we will add a home page to our site, create a syllabus page from a Word document, and delete the WordPress sample page.

Creating a home page

By default, our site's home page displays our ten most recent posts. While this is the desired format for a blog, it may be more appropriate for a course website to display a more traditional static home page.

To begin with, create a new page by hovering over **Pages** in the WordPress left sidebar and choose the **Add New** option. Title this new page Home by typing in the **Enter title here** text area. On this page, we can add content as desired, such as a brief summary of our class or any other information we wish to immediately convey.

We may also wish to include a link to our department or school website. To do so, type the text that will display as our link, such as For more information, visit our department's website.

To create a link, highlight the text that will become our link, and click on the **Insert/ Edit Link** button (which appears as a chain link). This will open a modal box that will gray out the rest of the screen. Insert the full web address of the page you would like to link to in the link **URL**. The link **Title** is not required, but if the text link is not descriptive enough (such as a link where it simply says **click here**), a title can be greatly beneficial to students with disabilities who may use screen-reading software. For the **Title**, enter a simple, descriptive phrase, such as English Department Site. We may also check the **Open link in a new window/tab** checkbox, if we wish for students to remain on our site while visiting the link.

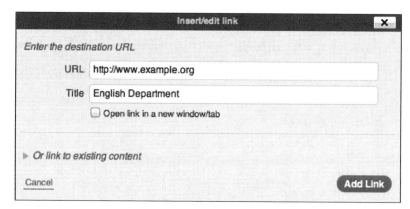

Once we are satisfied with our page, we may publish it by clicking on the blue **Publish** button.

Page order

As we create our site's pages, we will most likely want the home page to appear first in the site's navigation. By default, all pages are given an order of 0 and sorted alphabetically. Leaving our home page order at 0, we can then assign our other pages higher numerical values to organize our navigation. As we create the sample pages of our site, I will recommend a page order to reorganize the navigation order.

Making the Home page static

Though we have created a page titled **Home**, you may notice when previewing the site that our posts still act as the actual home page of our site.

In order to change this we must first create an empty page to hold our posts.

1. Create a new page.
2. Title the page something descriptive such as `Blog`.
3. Leave the content of the page empty.
4. Set the page order to `1`, so that it is the second item in our navigation.
5. Click on the **Publish** button.

Once our empty **Blog** page has been created, we must adjust our site's **Reading Settings** to display a static home page.

1. Hover over **Settings** and choose **Reading**.
2. In the **Front page displays** option, select the **A static page** radio button.
3. For the **Front page**, select the **Home** option from the drop-down menu.
4. For the **Posts page**, select our empty **Blog** page.

Home will now appear as our site's static home page while our posts will appear on the **Blog** page.

Syllabus page

One of the most common pages of any course site is the course syllabus. Most educators have written and formatted their syllabus in Microsoft Word or a similar Word processor. Using the **Paste from Word** feature of WordPress we can easily preserve our syllabus formatting.

To create our **Syllabus** page, hover over the **+ New** button in the WordPress admin bar at the top of the screen and choose **Page**. This will take us to the **New Page** WordPress screen. Title the new page `Syllabus` by typing in the page title textbox.

To use **Paste from Word**:

From your Word processor, select and copy the appropriate text.

1. In WordPress, click on the **Show/Hide Kitchen Sink** button in the text editor.
2. Click on the **Paste From Word** button that displays in the newly appeared second row.
3. Paste the text into the **Paste from Word** textbox.
4. Click on the **Insert** button.

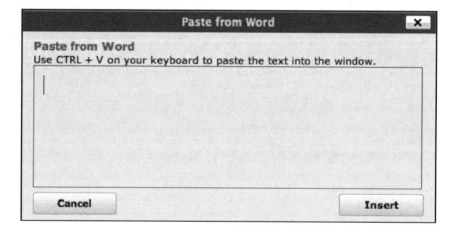

While the **Paste from Word** feature will preserve much of the basic formatting of a Word document, the results are not always ideal. If the document requires cleaning up or is not being pasted directly from a Word document, the basic editing and formatting of posts act very similar to that of most Word processing applications. If in doubt, consult the WordPress support page for formatting in the visual editor (`http://en.support.wordpress.com/visual-editor/`).

Before publishing the page, set the **Order** to 2 so that it will appear after **Home** and **Blog** in our site's navigation.

Deleting the sample page

Similar to our "Hello World" post, WordPress comes with a sample page (appropriately titled `Sample Page`). To delete this page from our site, hover over the **Pages** in the left sidebar, and select the **All Pages** option. WordPress will present us with a list of our site's pages. Hover over the **Sample Page** and choose the **Trash** option to delete it.

Posts

Regularly writing posts will keep students updated on the latest course news, assignments, and supplemental course materials. In this section we will create a new post that contains a video, update our site's **Hello World** post, and keep our posts organized by using categories and tags.

Adding a video to a post

WordPress has made embedding videos from popular media sites such as YouTube or Vimeo a straightforward process. To begin, create a new post by hovering over the **+ New** button in the admin toolbar and click on the **Post** button. Enter a descriptive title for the post within the title box.

To embed the video from popular video services, click on the **HTML** tab above the post editor and paste the URL of the video's web page into the new post. Optionally, press on *Return* key, click on the **Visual** tab to return to the visual editor, and type a corresponding message for the post.

The following screenshot shows our video post as it appears in the WordPress Post editor:

The following screenshot shows the YouTube video post as it appears on our site:

Categories and tags

Assigning post **Categories** is a good way to organize and provide context for our posts. **Categories** are a means of classifying posts and are one of the key differentiators between posts and pages. Using categories can help students and site users easily find relevant and related information. By default WordPress assigns each post a category of **Uncategorized**. To add a category, type a category name of your choosing within the **Categories** box. As this post contains supplemental course material, we can assign it a **Supplemental** category.

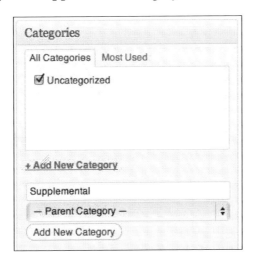

In addition to our category, we can tag our post. While tags are similar to categories, they function as the specific keywords of an individual post. The use of tags can help organize small pieces of information across our site. As the sample post contains a video interview of an author discussing his book, our tags may be: `video`, `interview`, `author name`, and `book title`.

To add tags to a post, type the tag words into the **Tags** box with each tag separated by a comma.

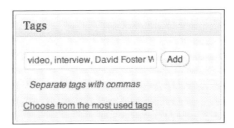

Clicking on the **Preview** button from within the **Publish** box allows us to see how the post will appear on our site. If necessary, we can then return to the post editor to make additional adjustments or edits. Once the post is complete and ready to be published to the site, click on the blue **Publish** button.

Editing an existing post and adding an image

By hovering over **Posts** in the left sidebar and choosing the **All Posts** option, we are able to see a list of each of our posts. By default WordPress comes with a single pre-written post, titled **Hello World**. Clicking on the name of the post will take us to the **Edit Post** page, allowing us to make changes to this post.

Since this is our site's first post, we may wish to keep it, but edit the post contents to serve as a more accurate introduction. To begin, edit the text with an appropriate welcome message for your students.

Adding an image

To add an image to this post, click on the **Upload/Insert media** icon directly above the post editor. We will be prompted to drag-and-drop files into the **Add Media** area or we may click on the **Select Files** button to find the appropriate image on our computer. Once the image has been uploaded, WordPress will allow us to edit the image or image options before placing it into our post.

> Occasionally WordPress users will receive an error stating that the web server did not have permission to write to the uploads directory when attempting to upload an image or file for the first time. If you receive this error, consult the WordPress Codex for how to change file permissions (http://codex.wordpress.org/Changing_File_Permissions).

Clicking on the **Edit Image** button will provide us with options to crop, rotate, or flip our image.

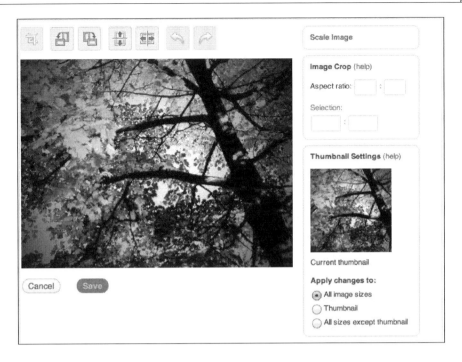

We can also adjust the **Title, Alternate Text, Caption, Description, Link URL, Alignment**, and **Size**. I would recommend always including **Alternate Text** for the image. **Alternate Text** should provide a brief description of the image for those who may have difficulty seeing it. This will increase the accessibility of our site for students and readers who are visually impaired and use a screen reader to access the information.

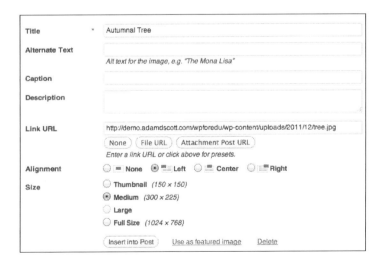

Note that size of the image is controlled by the media settings or may be set by the theme.

Once we have entered any necessary information and made any desired edits, we can add the image to our post by clicking on the **Insert into Post** button.

Before publishing the post, add an appropriate category such as **Course News**.

To preview our updated post, click on the **Preview Changes** button within the **Publish** box. If we are happy with our edited post, we can click on the **Update** button within the **Publish** box to post the newly revised version to our site.

Editing post categories

As mentioned previously, assigning post **Categories** is a good way to organize and provide context for our posts. **Categories** can be seen as a means of classifying posts. Using categories can help students and site users easily find relevant and related information.

By default WordPress assigns each post a category of **Uncategorized**. The WordPress **Categories** page allows us to manage and edit our post categories.

Changing the default WordPress category

The default WordPress category is **Uncategorized**, which will automatically be applied to all of our posts unless specified otherwise. We are able to change the default post category within our site's **Writing Settings** page.

From anywhere within WordPress, hover over **Posts** in the left sidebar and choose **Categories** from the drop-down menu. To add an additional category, enter a category name and click on the **Add New Category** button.

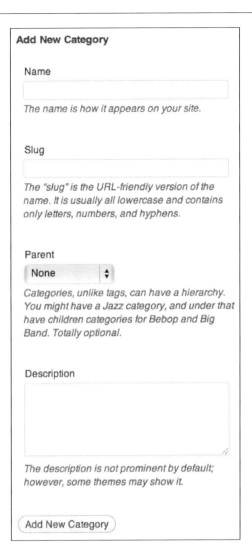

Optionally, we may also choose to add a **Slug**, **Parent**, or **Description** for the category. The **Slug** is a URL-friendly version of the category and by default will be all lowercase and free of spaces and symbols. If left blank, WordPress will automatically generate an appropriate slug for each category. For example, a category titled `Research Paper` will receive a category slug of `research-paper`.

The **Parent** drop-down menu allows us to create sub-categories that belong beneath other categories. For example, we may have a parent category entitled **Assignment** and create child categories titled **Essay, Reading,** and **Research Paper**.

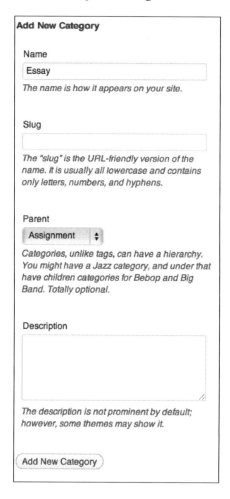

If we choose, we may also enter a brief **Description** of the category, which is utilized by some WordPress themes.

By creating a variety of categories now, we can easily select an appropriate category when writing each post. For our sample site, the categories I have created are:

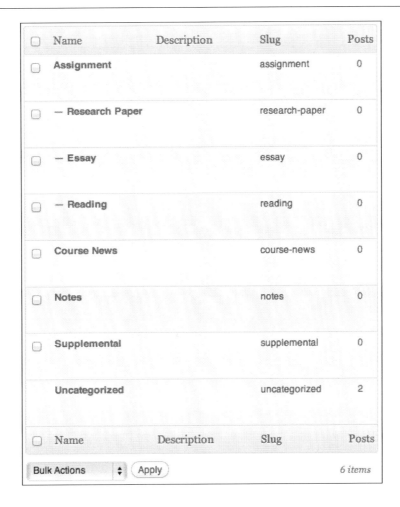

	Name	Description	Slug	Posts
☐	**Assignment**		assignment	0
☐	— Research Paper		research-paper	0
☐	— Essay		essay	0
☐	— Reading		reading	0
☐	**Course News**		course-news	0
☐	**Notes**		notes	0
☐	**Supplemental**		supplemental	0
	Uncategorized		uncategorized	2
☐	Name	Description	Slug	Posts

Bulk Actions ⬍ (Apply)   *6 items*

Themes

One of the advantages of using a content management system such as WordPress is
that the site's content is separated from the visual design. Because of this, we are able
to easily update the look of our site.

Themes is the term WordPress uses to describe the templates that control the
appearance of our site. All new WordPress sites use a theme entitled Twenty Eleven.

Due to the popularity of WordPress there are currently well over a thousand free
themes available through WordPress.org. Additionally, there are hundreds of
premium themes for sale around the web.

We can easily search for and install free themes from within the WordPress interface. To add themes, hover over the **Appearance** tab in the left sidebar and choose the **Themes** option. This will present us with the **Manage Themes** screen. To search for new themes, click on the **Install Themes** tab at the top of the page. From here we can choose to search for themes, upload our own theme, or browse through the featured and recently uploaded themes.

The **Manage Themes** screen allows us to see all of the themes we have installed. From this screen we may choose to **Activate**, **Preview**, or **Delete** any of the themes we have downloaded. When we **Activate** a theme, it will become the current, active theme of our public WordPress site.

Here is how the sample course site appears using the free theme `picochic` by Valentin:

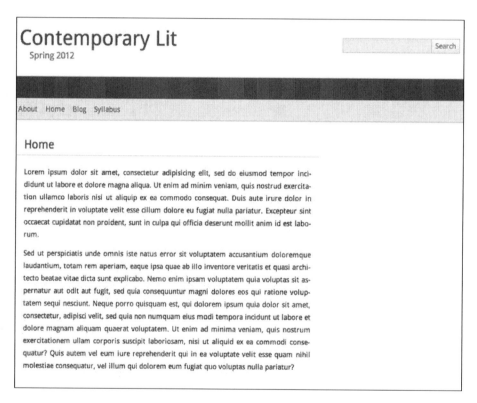

Widgets

Widgets are small pieces of functionality or content that can be added to specific areas of our site. WordPress offers a variety of widgets including category lists, links, recent comments, text areas, tag clouds, and a search box. These widgets can be added to any widget-ready area of our site.

The most common widget area is a sidebar, though many themes support a variety of other widget ready areas, including the header and footer. The widget areas will vary based on what is supported by the active theme.

To access the **Widget** screen, hover over the **Appearance** tab and choose the **Widgets** field. The **Available Widgets** page appears in the main area of the screen. The available widget areas are seen in the right sidebar. To add a widget, click-and-drag the available widget to the desired widget area.

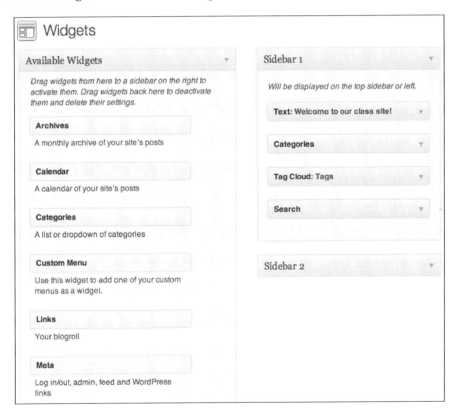

In our sample course site, I've chosen to add several widgets:

- **Text** to add an additional text area to the page sidebar. This can be useful to detail class information such as the meeting time or a short description of the course.

- **Recent Posts** to display a list of our site's recent posts. This will present students with a list of the headlines of our most recent course news. This is particularly useful when using a static home page, such as in our example.

- **Categories** to display a list of our site's categories. By displaying a list of categories, students can quickly access all of the posts that cover a specific category of information, such as **Assignments**.

- **Tag cloud** to display a list of our site's tags. The tag cloud will organize related posts, which will help students to sort through the information on our site.

- **Search** to add a search box to our site. Adding a search area will aid students in finding the information they need.

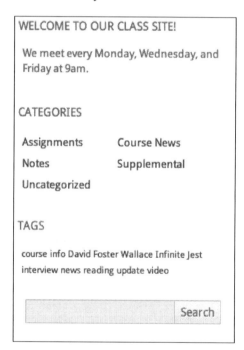

Menus

The WordPress menu feature allows us to create a custom navigation menu for our site. By default, WordPress creates navigation links for each new page, but we are able to create a custom menu that also includes post categories and links to other websites.

To create a menu, form the WordPress dashboard, hover over the **Appearance** tab in the left sidebar and choose the **Menus** tab. Enter a name for the menu and click on the blue **Create Menu** button.

Select the pages to add to the menu within the **Pages** box on the left side of the screen and click on the **Add to Menu** button. Because this menu will most likely be replacing the site's default navigation it is a good idea to select all of the pages.

To add a post category to the navigation menu, click on the appropriate checkbox within the **Categories** box and click on the **Add to Menu** button. In the case of our course site, adding the **Assignment** category will give our students quick access to all assignment posts on the site.

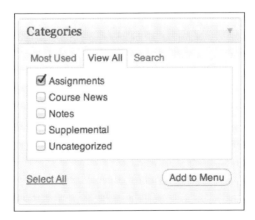

To add outside links, such as a department or school website, enter the site's URL and title within the **Custom Links** box and click on the **Add to Menu** button.

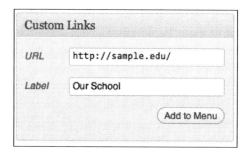

Once the menu is complete, choose the menu name within the **Theme Locations** drop-down box and click on the **Save** button.

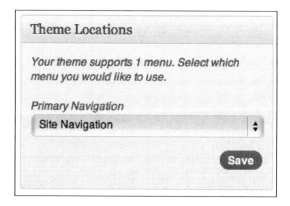

We may rearrange the menu items within the main area of the screen by dragging the navigation elements into the desired order. Once the menu is complete, click on the blue **Save Menu** button.

Our custom menu as it appears on our site will look like the following screenshot:

Summary

Through this chapter we've taken a closer look at Pages and Posts by exploring the visual editor, publishing options, categories, and tags. We created a page titled **Home** and set it as the static home page of our site as well as a **Syllabus** page with content copied and pasted from a Word processor. We updated a post with an image and new text and wrote a new post that includes an embedded video.

Additionally, we gave our site a fresh look by searching for and installing a new theme. With our new theme in place, we added additional content and functionality using widgets and created a custom menu for improved navigation.

In the next chapter we will look at the use of WordPress plugins to enhance the functionality of our site.

3

Enhancing WordPress with Plugins

With our basic site structure put into place, we can now use plugins to greatly increase the versatility of WordPress. Plugins are bits of code, typically written by third-party developers that add extra functionality to WordPress. These plugins typically add a specific ability to a site, such as a contact form or an event calendar.

In this chapter, we will explore how to find and install WordPress plugins. I will also provide you with a list of plugins that are applicable in an education setting.

Finding and installing plugins

Much like themes, plugins can be found and installed from within the WordPress administration interface. Hover over the **Plugins** tab in the left sidebar and choose the **Add New** tab. We are then presented with the **Install Plugins** page.

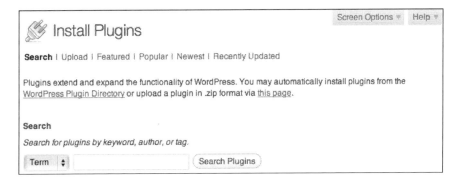

From the **Install Plugins** page, we are able to **Search** for plugins or **Upload** our own as well as browse the **Featured**, **Popular**, **Newest**, and **Recently Updated** plugins. Browsing the **Featured** and **Popular** categories is a great way to get a feel for the kinds of functionality made possible by plugins.

Once we find a plugin that interests us, we may click the **Details** link to learn more about it. To install the plugin, click on the **Install Now** link. In the following example, I have chosen to install the WordPress Jetpack plugin. This plugin adds a variety of additional functionality such as spellcheck, site statistics, e-mail subscriptions, and more.

> **Jetpack by WordPress.com**
> Details | Install Now

WordPress will then download and unzip the plugin file to our server. Once it is complete, we will be given the option to either **Activate the Plugin** or **Return to Plugin Installer**. Activating will essentially turn the plugin on, while choosing to return to the plugin installer will leave the plugin installed but inactive.

 If you encounter problems while installing or managing plugins, consult the WordPress Codex (`http://codex.wordpress.org/Managing_Plugins`).

 Installing Plugin: Jetpack by WordPress.com 1.2.2

Downloading install package from `http://downloads.wordpress.org/plugin/jetpack.1.2.2.zip`...

Unpacking the package...

Installing the plugin...

Successfully installed the plugin **Jetpack by WordPress.com 1.2.2**.

Activate Plugin | Return to Plugin Installer

Managing plugins

By hovering over **Plugins** and choosing the **Installed Plugins** options, we are able to see the list of plugins we have installed.

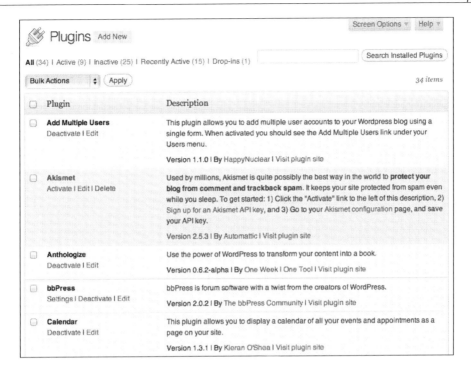

From the previous screenshot, we are able to **Activate**, **Deactivate**, and **Delete** our Plugins. We also see a brief description of each plugin, its version number, and a link to **Visit plugin site**. Visiting the plugin's site is a great way to see instructions for how to use the plugin within WordPress.

Even after a plugin is activated, there are often settings or other steps to be completed before we see its changes live on our site. These settings will vary by plugin. Instructions for each plugin can be found either through the **Plugins** page at WordPress.org (http://wordpress.org/extend/plugins) or the plugin developer's website. Most plugins will display a **Settings** link below the plugin name on the **Plugins** page to allow us to quickly access its settings.

Plugins

There are thousands of WordPress plugins available, each designed to add a unique functionality to WordPress. In this section, I will cover a few of the plugins that are useful in an education setting. To find and install these plugins, visit the **Add New Plugins** page within WordPress and search for them by name.

Preinstalled WordPress plugins

WordPress comes with two plugins pre-installed, Hello Dolly and Akismet. The Hello Dolly plugin was created by Matt Mulenweg, the founding developer of WordPress, while Akismet is developed and maintained by Automattic, the company behind the commercially hosted `WordPress.com`. While these plugins come pre-installed with every new WordPress installation, they are not activated and there is no requirement to do so.

Hello Dolly

Hello Dolly is a fun plugin that adds a random lyric from *Hello, Dolly* to the admin screen. While this plugin may not have a practical application for a WordPress site, it allows us to grow in comfort activating or deactivating plugins.

Akismet

For sites that allow comments, it is a good idea to use the Akismet plugin. Akismet is a plugin designed to prevent comment spam. According to `Akismet.com`, there have been well over forty billion spam blog comments, while there have only been five billion legitimate comments. If you have ever had a blog, you are most likely familiar with the overwhelming amount of spam that can accumulate within the comment section. Akismet automatically detects and filters out these spam comments.

To use Akismet:

1. Activate the plugin.
2. Click on the **You must enter your Akismet API key** for it to work link that appears at the top of the screen or the **Akismet Configuration** link within **Plugins** in the left sidebar menu.
3. Obtain an API key by following the **Get Your Key** link to `http://akismet.com/WordPress`.
4. Choose a donation amount and follow the steps to create an API key.
5. Once we have an API key, we can return to our WordPress installation, paste the key into the **Akismet Configuration** box, and click on the **Update options** button.

Akismet Configuration

Akismet is almost ready. You must enter your Akismet API key for it to work.

For many people, Akismet will greatly reduce or even completely eliminate the comment and trackback spam you get on your site. If one does happen to get through, simply mark it as "spam" on the moderation screen and Akismet will learn from the mistakes. If you don't have an API key yet, you can get one at Akismet.com.

Akismet API Key

Please enter an API key. (Get your key.)

(What is this?)

☐ Auto-delete spam submitted on posts more than a month old.

☐ Show the number of comments you've approved beside each comment author.

(Update options »)

The Cost of Akismet

Akismet is free for non-profit, personal use, though we may choose to give a donation towards the continued development of this plugin. Akismet also offers a "Pro" plan for $5 per month with expanded features for personal users. Businesses or large institutions looking to employ Akismet will have to pay a larger fee, beginning at $50 per month.

With Akismet installed, we should see a significant decrease in the amount of spam comments and trackbacks that appear on our site.

Education plugins

As the use of WordPress in education continues to grow, many third-party developers have created plugins specific to the needs of educators.

ScholarPress Courseware

ScholarPress Courseware is one of the most fully-featured education plugins available. In fact, a later chapter of this book will be dedicated to using the BuddyPress Courseware plugin. However, for users not interested in the social features of BuddyPress, the ScholarPress Courseware plugin still offers many benefits.

ScholarPress Courseware allows us to easily create a course schedule, post course assignments, and develop a course bibliography. This plugin was designed with higher education in mind, but could certainly be useful in a wide range of education settings. The plugin will create two new pages on our site, Bibliography and Schedule.

ScholarPress Courseware allows us to create a schedule of upcoming classes or assignment due dates.

The bibliography tool is designed to keep track of the books, articles, websites, videos, and more that are referenced in the class.

The **Assignment** page allows us to add detailed assignment information, which will then be posted to the **Schedule** page.

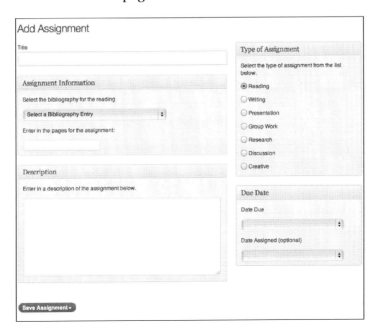

WP Survey and Quiz Tool

The WP Survey and Quiz Tool plugin enables us to create quizzes, surveys, and polls with an unlimited number of questions. Quiz questions can take on multiple formats including multiple choice, single answer, and free text.

To use the WP Survey and Quiz Tool to create a quiz:

1. Install and activate the WP Survey and Quiz Tool plugin.

2. Click on **WPSQT** in the left WordPress sidebar.

3. Click on the **Add New Quiz** link at the top of the screen.

4. Give the quiz a name and click on the **Save Quiz** button.

5. In order to add questions, we must create at least one section in our quiz. Add as many sections as necessary to separate and organize the quiz content. Once we have finished adding sections, click on the **Save** button.

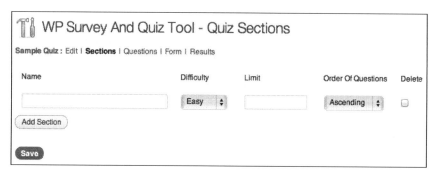

6. To add quiz questions, click on the **Question** link to visit the **Questions** page. Click on the **Add New Question** button from the **Questions** page.

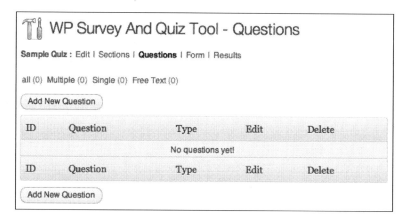

7. Add a new question and select the type of response for the question (multiple choice, drop-down, or free text).

8. For multiple choice and drop-down questions, enter the possible responses.

9. Once the question is complete, click on the **Save Question** button.

10. Continue adding questions as needed.

Once the quiz is complete, we will need to post it to our site. To embed the quiz, create a new page and add `[wpsqt_quiz name=""]` to the body of the page. Within the quotes enter the name of the quiz. For a quiz titled *Quiz 1*, the embed code would appear as `[wpsqt_quiz name="Quiz 1"]`.

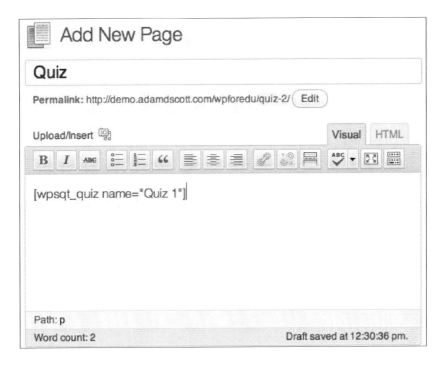

To view quiz results, hover over **WPSQT** in the sidebar and select the **Quizzes** option. Hovering over the name of a quiz will present us with a **Results** link. From the **Results** screen hover over the individual quiz title and click on the **Mark** link to access and assess the submitted answers.

ID	Title	Score	Percentage	Pass/Fail	Status	Date
3	**Anonymous - ::1** Mark l Delete	Unable to auto mark	Unable to auto mark	Fail	Unviewed	24-04-12 19:34:17

If students are not registered users of your WordPress site, be sure to add a **free text** question requesting the student name. To learn more about user registration, consult the WordPress Codex (`http://codex.wordpress.org/Users_Add_New_Screen`).

Grader

Grader is a plugin that allows site administrators to assign grades to individual posts through the post comments. The grade is only visible to the site administrator and post author. This is useful for a site where students are given accounts and contribute to the site with posts.

To assign a grade, the site administrator leaves a comment on the student written post beginning with the text **@grade**.

Using the **@grade** token creates a private comment that will only be visible to the site administrator and post author.

Conversation and communication plugins

A WordPress site allows us to facilitate better communication between the instructor and students as well as encouraging student discussion. There are a number of plugins that add contact forms, improve the WordPress commenting system, and even add the ability to incorporate a discussion forum into our site.

Contact Form 7

Contact Form 7 allows us to add a simple contact form to our site. This will allow students and site visitors to easily contact a course instructor through e-mail. Contact Form 7 is typically one of the first plugins I install on any WordPress site.

To use Contact Form 7:

1. Install and activate the Contact Form 7 plugin.

2. Click on **Contact** in the left WordPress sidebar to visit the **contact form** settings page.

3. The default contact form requests the sender's name, e-mail address, an e-mail subject, and an e-mail message. From this screen we can add fields to the form, edit the e-mail recipient, and change the e-mail message.

4. To add the form to a page, copy the embed code at the top of the screen.

5. Create a new page titled **Contact**, edit any existing page, or add a text widget and paste the contact form embed code.

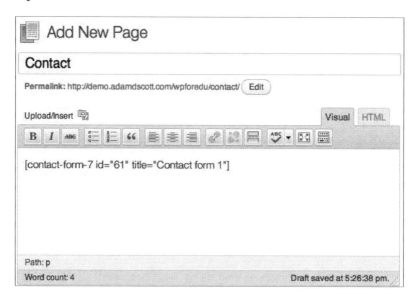

Semi-Private Comments

With the Semi-Private Comments plugin enabled, site visitors will only be able to see the comments they themselves leave as well as those of the site administrator. This works by detecting a site visitor's IP address and only displaying the comments that have been made at that address. This plugin can be useful in scenarios where we want to encourage users to leave comments, but not for the use of discussion. Ensuring student privacy with the Semi-Private Comments plugin can lead to authentic student responses.

Please note that environments where users' IP addresses change often, such as Wi-Fi networks or computer lab environments, can cause the IP address detection of the plugin to be less effective. In this scenario, the plugin also has the ability to work with registered WordPress users.

IntenseDebate Comments

The IntenseDebate Comments plugin is in direct contrast to Semi-Private Comments, as it aims to increase discussion within the WordPress comment section. It works by allowing users to easily reply to comments, to *like* or *dislike* other comments, and subscribe to a comment thread through e-mail or popular RSS readers.

To set up IntenseDebate Comments, install and activate the IntenseDebate Comments plugin, visit the **IntenseDebate** page within the WordPress **Settings** and sign in to your WordPress.com account.

Disqus

Similar to IntenseDebate Comments, Disqus provides an enhanced commenting system for our WordPress site. Disqus is used by popular websites such as CNN and Time.

Disqus allows us to:

- Collect and display Twitter tweets that mention a post from our siteDisplay comments in real time
- Embed media, such as images or video into comments
- Create a list of restricted words that cannot appear within the comments
- Have greater control over our site's comments with advanced comment moderation tools

In order to use Disqus on our site:

1. Create an account at disqus.com.
2. Install and activate the Disqus plugin.
3. Click on the **configure the plugin** link or hover over **Comments** in the sidebar and choose the **Disqus** option.
4. Log in with your Disqus account.
5. Click the link to register a new site on the Disqus website.
6. Follow the instructions on the Disqus website and select the appropriate commenting features.
7. Return to your WordPress dashboard and select your domain from the Disqus settings page.

bbPress

The bbPress plugin installs a lightweight discussion forum to our site. This is a great way for students to ask questions and respond to each other's ideas. In order for others to post, they will need to be registered site users. This can be done from the **Users** page or using the **Add Multiple Users** plugin mentioned later in the chapter.

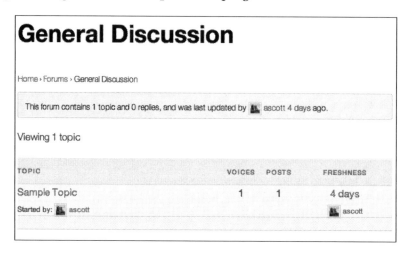

Social plugins

It's no secret that students frequently engage in social networking. Adding course content to social networks is a great way to engage students. There are a number of WordPress plugins that allow us to easily incorporate social networks into our site.

WP to Twitter

WP to Twitter will automatically tweet anytime a new post is created. The plugin has a number of additional settings such as the ability to use a post's tags as hashtags and appending text to any tweet.

Simple Facebook Connect

Simple Facebook Connect is a WordPress plugin that incorporates a wide range of Facebook integration into our site. Most importantly, the plugin will automatically post blog updates to a Facebook profile or fan page. One of the more interesting features is that the plugin will integrate comments left at `Facebook.com` back into our WordPress posts.

Other Plugins

There are many other plugins that can improve the functionality of our WordPress site and increase student engagement. Using plugins we are able to incorporate event calendars, create a mobile version of our site, easily add WordPress users, and export our site's contents as a digital book.

Jetpack

Depending on your web host, you may have seen banner ads throughout your WordPress installation advising you to employ the *cloud-powered features* of the Jetpack plugin. Jetpack allows us to add features to a self-hosted WordPress site that were previously only available to `WordPress.com` users.

The Jetpack plugin adds many additional features including:

- Installation of the Latex markup language, for writing math equations and formulas
- Site visitor statistics
- Spelling and grammar checks within the Post and Page editors
- The ability for site visitors to subscribe to new posts through e-mail
- A share button, allowing site visitors to easily share our posts through popular social networking sites
- Additional sidebar widgets, such as the ability to display images or a feed of Twitter updates
- The ability to easily create shortened URLs
- Pop-up gravatars for site authors and commenters
- The ability to easily embed media from a range of popular sites

To use Jetpack with our site, we will first need an account at `WordPress.com`. When signing up at `WordPress.com`, click on the **signup for just a username** link from the account sign up page. This will prevent us from creating an unnecessary blog.

To use Jetpack on our site:

1. Activate the **Jetpack** plugin from our **Plugins** page.
2. Click on the **Jetpack** link in the WordPress sidebar.
3. Click on the **Connect to WordPress.com** link and enter your `WordPress.com` username and password.

4. We may then configure each individual Jetpack feature from the **Jetpack** page by clicking on the **Configure** button.

Calendar

The Calendar plugin incorporates an event calendar into our site. With an event calendar, we are able to list assignment due dates, class meeting times, exams, and more.

To add events to the calendar and manage calendar categories, visit the **Calendar** link in the left sidebar.

Once events have been added to the calendar, we can add it to a page by typing {CALENDAR} into the body of the page.

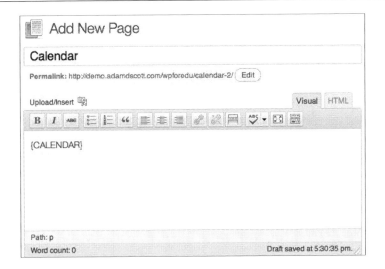

The calendar appears on our page as shown in the following screenshot:

In addition to the full page calendar, there is also an upcoming events widget that will display a list of upcoming events within any widget area of our site.

WordPress Mobile Pack

Mobile web browsing is growing at a rapid pace. There are currently 1.3 billion page views from mobile devices per year (http://www.zeldman.com/2011/12/14/why-mobile/). Some WordPress themes will nicely scale down to a mobile view, but for those that do not, there are several plugins that will create a mobile optimized version of our site.

Responsive design

When browsing for WordPress themes, look for those labeled as *responsive*. Responsively designed websites scale to the size of a user's device. These themes will not require a mobile site plugin such as WordPress Mobile Pack.

WordPress Mobile Pack is one plugin that adds a mobile theme to your site. Site visitors will have the option of viewing the desktop version, if they prefer. The plugin also allows us to choose which widgets should appear in the mobile version of our site. The plugin also comes with four different color schemes, allowing us to roughly match the look of our desktop site.

Add Multiple Users for WordPress

If you are interested in allowing students to publish posts and content to your WordPress site or use the bbPress forums, Add Multiple Users for WordPress is an incredible time saver. This plugin allows us to add up to 50 users at a time, simply by entering names, e-mail addresses, and assigning a username.

Anthologize

Anthologize is a plugin that allows us to format the content of our site into an electronic book in ePub, PDF, TEI, or RTF format. Using this tool, we can easily export our site as an e-book. This is a handy way to archive student work or prepare a document for future classes.

Updating plugins

Plugin authors will frequently update their plugins to fix bugs, add compatibility for WordPress updates, or add additional features. When updates are available for a plugin a number will appear next to **Plugins** in the WordPress sidebar.

To update plugins:

1. Visit the **Updates** page by hovering over **Dashboard** in the left sidebar and click on the **Updates** button.
2. Click on the checkbox next to the plugin to be updated.
3. Click on the **Update Plugins** button.

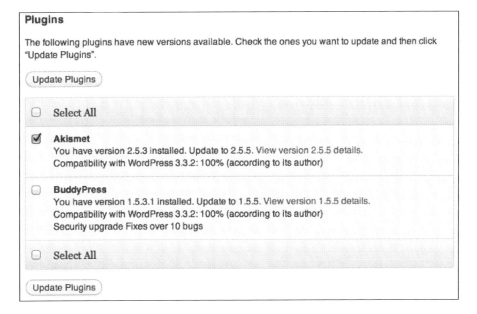

 It is possible to update all plugins at once by clicking on the **Select All** checkbox, however updating plugins one at a time can aid in troubleshooting plugin related issues.

Uninstalling plugins

We are able to uninstall unused plugins from our WordPress site. To uninstall plugins:

1. Visit the **Plugins** page.

2. Click on the **Deactivate** link below the plugin name.

3. Once the plugin is deactivated, click on the **Delete** link below the plugin name.

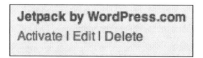

Deleting plugins typically deletes configuration information and data that has been created by the plugin. Use caution when deleting a plugin that you have made significant use of.

Summary

Through this chapter, we've looked at the use of WordPress plugins as a way to enhance a site's functionality. We've searched for, installed, activated, deactivated, and deleted plugins. We've also looked at a number of plugins to provide a practical application in an education environment.

In the next chapter we will explore the WordPress multisite feature, which allows us to create and manage a network of WordPress sites.

Enabling a Multisite Network

4

The multisite feature allows us to create a network of WordPress sites. This feature is ideal for setting up student blogs and portfolios or creating a network of sites for instructors and teachers. A WordPress network is a group of individual sites on one shared instance of WordPress. With our multisite network, we act as the administrator, creating and controlling the accounts and sites.

In a WordPress network, each user receives his or her own WordPress installation, but no a shared codebase with a limited set of plugins and themes. A WordPress multisite network is different from multiauthor blogs, where multiple users are given access to a single site.

I have personally used WordPress multisite networks as a means of managing student blogs and portfolios. I have found blogs to be an effective way for students to curate and share class resources and links as well as an open space for students to write brief reflections on course content. WordPress acts as an effective portfolio tool, allowing students to create pages and posts containing a selection of work from the class. A multisite network serves as also an effective way to create department-wide websites, providing each faculty member his/her own site while only the site administrator is responsible for managing and updating the WordPress installation.

In this chapter, we will step through the process of creating a WordPress network. Once the network is installed, we will add sites, explore network management, share themes, and plugins across the network, more easily manage the network with plugins, and display network content on our site.

Before installing

The server requirements of a WordPress network are the same as those needed to power an individual WordPress site. It is important to be aware that the additional sites created by the network will increase the amount of bandwidth used as well as the size of the database. If the network is larger than a few sites, contact the hosting company to ensure that your hosting package will be able to handle the extra load.

When creating a network, there are two types of site URLs from which we can choose:

- Sub-domain URLs are domain based and create URLs such as:
  `http://samplestudent.example.org`
- Sub-directory URLs networks are path based and create URLs such as:
  `http://example.org/samplestudent`

In order to use the sub-domain option, we must make changes at the server or hosting level and update the DNS configuration. For this reason, I recommend using the sub-directory option. The only requirement of the sub-directory network is that our primary site is already using permalinks, as discussed in *Chapter 1, Installing and Configuring WordPress*.

To turn permalinks on, visit **Settings | Permalinks** and select one of the **Common Settings**. I would recommend using the **Month and name** permalink setting.

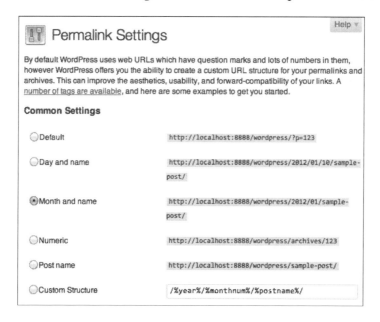

> If you choose to create a network from an existing WordPress site it is a good idea to first back up your site's database. Backups are covered in greater detail in *Chapter 7, Site Management*.

Creating the network

It is possible to create a multisite network manually and those who are interested in doing so may consult the **Create A Network** page of the WordPress Codex (http://codex.wordpress.org/Create_A_Network) for detailed instructions. For those who are less comfortable working with code, developer Jason Grim has created a plugin entitled **Enable Multi-Site** that will take care of the heavy lifting involved with setting up a multisite network.

To create a network with the **Enable Multi-Site** plugin:

1. Visit the **Install Plugins** page and search for the **Enable Multi-Site** plugin.

2. Install and activate the plugin.

3. Go to **Settings | Enable Multi-Site** to visit the **Enable Multi-Site** page, which is shown in the following screenshot:

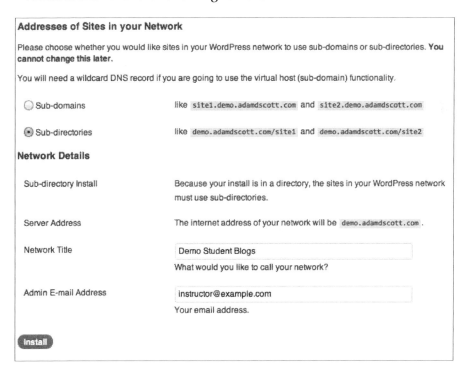

4. Select the **Sub-directories** option.

5. Complete the **Network Details** by naming the network and entering your e-mail address.

6. Click on the **Install** button to create the multisite network.

7. Once the installation is complete, we will need to log out of WordPress and log back in to access the new network features.

Exploring the Network Admin area

With multisite enabled, we now have access to the **Network Admin** area of WordPress. From the **Network Admin** we are able to manage our network's settings, add or remove new sites, and manage themes and plugins.

To access the **Network Admin** area of WordPress:

1. Log in to WordPress.

2. Hover over **My Sites** in the toolbar at the top of the screen.

3. Click on the **Network Admin** tab.

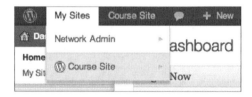

Once logged in to the **Network Admin** area, we see the network admin dashboard. The most notable difference between the **Network Admin** dashboard and that of our individual WordPress site is that the **Right Now** box presents us with an option to quickly add new sites or users rather than draft a new post.

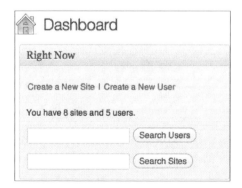

The left sidebar of the admin area allows us to navigate to the **Network Admin** screens.

- **Dashboard** returns us to our network admin dashboard
- **Sites** allows us to view our network's sites and add new sites to the network
- **Users** allows us to view our registered users and add additional users to the network
- **Themes** allows us to add, activate, and manage themes across the network
- **Plugins** allows us to add, activate, and manage plugins across the network
- **Settings** allows us to update our network's name, manage the registration settings, edit the welcome e-mail, edit the first post/page on new sites, control the amount of storage space for users, and set the default site language
- **Updates** allows us to update the WordPress installation, themes, and plugins for the network

Creating a new site

Creating a new site will provide a unique WordPress site for the specified recipient, such as a student or staff member. To create a new site from the **Network Admin Dashboard**, click on the **Create a New Site** link from the **Right Now** box. We may also create a new site from anywhere within the **Network Admin** area by hovering over **Sites** in the left sidebar and choosing the **Add New** option.

Once on the **Add New Site** page, complete the form by filling out the **Site Address**, **Site Title**, and **Admin Email**.

- **Site Address**: Enter the address of the new site into this text area. For a path based site, this would be the trailing slash. For example, if the new site was to be www.example.org/student1, simply enter student 1.

- **Site Title**: Give the site a title, such as the student or staff member's names

- **Admin Email**: The admin e-mail should be the e-mail address of the new site users

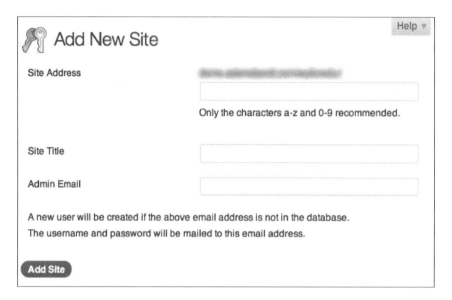

Once this is complete, the student or staff member will receive an e-mail with the site address as well as their login credentials. The user account will be the site address (such as student1) and the password will be randomly generated.

The first time a user logs in to their new site, they will not be prompted to create a new password. Instead, passwords can be changed by visiting the **Profile Page**.

To access the profile page:

1. Hover over the **user name/image** at the top left of the screen, in the WordPress admin bar

2. Choose the **Edit My Profile** option

3. Enter a new password

4. Click on the **Update Profile** button

We can change the e-mail message that new site owners receive from the **Network Admin Settings** menu. Adding instructions for how to update the user password will increase the likelihood that students will create a more memorable password.

Installing themes and plugins

Just as themes and plugins can be used to enhance our own site, they can add value to sites across our network. As the network administrator, we have control over which themes and plugins our users can enable.

The ability to determine the available plugins and themes is one of the key advantages of running a WordPress network. The site administrator can preselect the themes and plugins that will be most useful to network users. This is significantly different from a standalone WordPress installation, where the user has total control over themes and plugins.

Network enabled themes

Network users will not be able to search and install their own themes. Instead, network administrators will need to install a selection of themes for site users to choose from. This allows our users to personalize the look and feel of their WordPress site while providing the administrator with the ability to pre-approve or limit the use of themes. Users will also be able to change theme options such as widgets, allowing them to customize the look and feel of their site further.

To enable themes:

1. Log in to the **Network Admin** area.
2. Download and install themes as covered in *Chapter 2, Setting up our Class Site*.
3. Visit the **Installed Themes** page.
4. Click on the **Network Enable** link below each theme that should be enabled.

Alternately, we may also choose to bulk enable themes by selecting the theme checkbox and choosing **Network Enable** from the **Bulk Actions** drop-down menu.

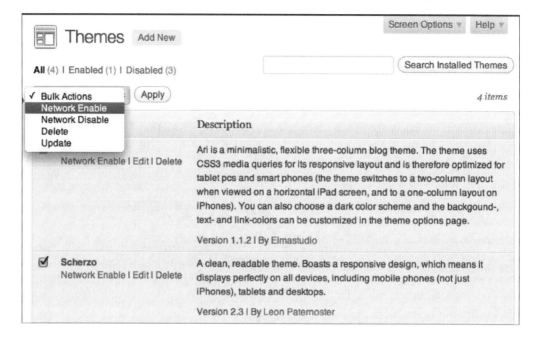

Network enabled plugins

Before network users are able to use plugins on their individual site, we must enable the plugin administration menu. This will allow users to see the plugin page from within their individual WordPress site. In order to do this:

1. Log in to the **Network Admin** area.
2. Visit the **Network Settings** page, by clicking on **Settings** in the left sidebar.
3. Scroll to the bottom of the screen and click on the checkbox next to **Plugins** in the **Menu Settings**.
4. Click on the **Save Changes** button.

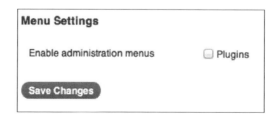

Once the plugin menu has been enabled for users, we can enable individual plugins across the network.

To enable plugins:

1. Log in to the **Network Admin** area.

2. Download and install plugins as covered in *Chapter 3, Enhancing WordPress with Plugins*.

3. Visit the **Installed Plugins** page.

4. Click on the **Network Activate** link below each plugin that you wish to enable.

Following these steps will install the plugin for all network sites. In order to actively use the plugin, users must still activate the plugin from their individual dashboard as described in *Chapter 3, Enhancing WordPress with Plugins*.

Network administrator plugins

In addition to enhancing the functionality of our public website, there are plugins designed to improve the experience of network administration. These plugins can provide network administrators with the ability to create new site templates, manage user plugins, and track activity across the network.

New Blog Templates

New Blog Templates (`http://premium.wpmudev.org/project/new-blog-template`) is a premium plugin by WPMU DEV. This plugin allows network administrators to create an empty template site, which can feature any pages, settings, plugins, content, and themes we wish. New sites can then be created using the template site as a basis, taking some of the initial workload from the user. This plugin is incredibly useful when developing student portfolios.

As a premium plugin, it is not free to download or available directly through our WordPress installation. To purchase and install the **New Blog Templates** plugin, visit the WPMU DEV website (`http://premium.wpmudev.org/project/new-blog-template/`) and follow their detailed instructions.

The popularity of WordPress has created a growing market for premium plugins and themes. Premium plugins and themes are those which developers choose to charge a fee for. They are typically sold either directly from the developer's website or from websites that act as plugin and theme marketplaces. These plugins and themes are not available through WordPress.org or directly from the WordPress dashboard.

Multisite Plugin Manager

Multisite Plugin Manager is a plugin that provides network administrators with greater control over plugins across the multisite installation. Using this plugin, the network administrator can choose to have plugins auto-activated for each new site, quickly assign plugin privileges, and mass activate/deactivate plugins across the network. This is a great tool for site administrators who anticipate their network users utilizing a large number of plugins.

Name	Version	Author	User Control	Mass Activate	Mass Deactivate
Calendar	1.3.1	Kieran O'Shea	Auto-Activate (All Users)	Activate All	Deactivate All
Community Gradebook	0.1	Manoj Chacko	None	Activate All	Deactivate All
Diamond MultiSite Widgets	1.8	Daniel Bozo	All Users	Activate All	Deactivate All

ThreeWP Activity Monitor

The ThreeWP Activity Monitor plugin provides the network administrator with the ability to track all activity across the network. The plugin adds an **Activity Monitor** page to the **Network Admin** site that displays the following:

- **User logins**
- **New posts**
- **New comments**
- **New pages**
- **Trashed pages, posts, and comments**
- **User changes**

Tracking this activity across the network provides us with a deeper understanding of how the network is being used.

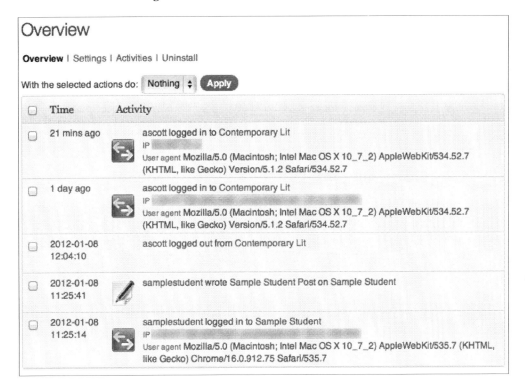

Network content

Displaying network content on our WordPress site is a great way to draw students and site visitors to the content published across the network. There are plugins available that allow us to display a list of network sites as well as generate a list of recent posts made from network sites. By displaying network content on our site, students are able to easily browse and access the work of their peers.

Displaying a list of network sites

The Multi-Site Site List Shortcode plugin creates a shortcode that when added to a page will display a list of links to all of the sites in the network. Once this plugin is installed and activated, add [site-list] to the body of a page to display the site list. For example, you might use this to create a *Students* page listing all of the individual student sites in the network. This would help students to connect with their classmates, promoting discussion and peer review of student posts.

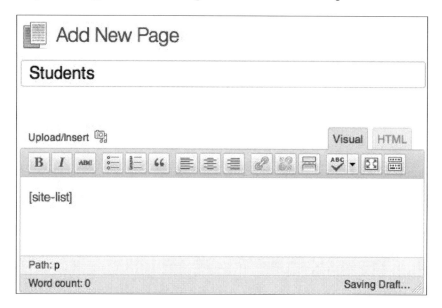

Displaying network posts

The Multisite Recent Posts Widget plugin adds a widget that will display a list of the most recent posts across our network. Using the Multisite Recent Posts Widget, we may choose the number of recent posts to display and give the list a title. While not feature rich, the Multisite Recent Posts Widget plugin is a simple solution for those who would like to display and link to the most recent network posts. By using this plugin, students are able to quickly scan the most recent posts created by their classmates and easily access those that they wish to read in full.

Summary

Creating a network allows us to give students or colleagues access to their own WordPress site. In this chapter we covered how to enable the WordPress multisite features. Once the network was created, we looked at how to create new sites, enable themes and plugins, use plugins to enhance the network administrator experience, and display network content on our own WordPress site.

In the next chapter we will use the BuddyPress plugin to create a fully-functioning social network.

5
Creating a Social Network with BuddyPress

A WordPress site is a great way for instructors to broadcast information to students, but is not ideal for student-to-student interaction. The BuddyPress plugin allows us to turn our course site into a fully-functioning social network. By employing BuddyPress as our social network, the site administrator has full control over the content and forms of communication that occur. This makes BuddyPress an ideal way to encourage online student collaboration.

I have used BuddyPress in courses where I would like to quickly share information with the class. I can post a link or file through the BuddyPress activity stream and students are able to access them in real time. BuddyPress also makes student research collaboration simpler, allowing students to easily share links and resources with their classmates.

By using BuddyPress, students and instructors have the ability to seamlessly communicate and collaborate with one another directly through the class site. In this chapter we'll cover how to install BuddyPress, use the BuddyPress activity feed, create student groups for collaboration, use the BuddyPress forum option, and protect the privacy of our students.

WordPress, Multisite, and BuddyPress

Throughout this book, we use several different versions of WordPress including a standard WordPress installation, WordPress Multisite Networks, and BuddyPress. The following table highlights the differences between these WordPress installations:

WordPress	The default WordPress installation creates a single blog site with a single user. It is possible to add additional users to the site, but all contributions, such as new posts and pages, will be made to the same site.
Multisite	The multisite feature creates a network of virtual sites from a single WordPress installation. Users are provided with their own WordPress site, which can also be controlled by the WordPress network administrator.
BuddyPress	BuddyPress is a WordPress plugin that turns a standard WordPress installation into a social network, enabling features for site users such as an activity feed and private messaging.
Multisite with BuddyPress	BuddyPress and Multisite networks can run from the same WordPress installation. In this scenario, the default WordPress site may act as the BuddyPress social network, while users will also have access to the individual WordPress sites of the network.

Installing BuddyPress

To install BuddyPress, first install and activate the BuddyPress plugin. To install the plugin, log in to the WordPress dashboard, hover over **Plugins** in the left sidebar and choose **Add New**. From the **Install Plugins** screen, search for and activate **BuddyPress** (http://wordpress.org/extend/plugins/buddypress/). At the time of writing, the current version of BuddyPress is 1.5.5.

 If you are installing BuddyPress in addition to the WordPress Multisite Network (as covered in *Chapter 4, Enabling a Multisite Network*), BuddyPress will be installed and managed from within the **Network Admin** dashboard. While possible to run both a multisite network and BuddyPress, I have encountered occasional compatibility issues. I would recommend choosing the one that best suits your site needs.

Once the plugin has been activated, we can follow the BuddyPress **Installation Wizard** to setup our social network. To access the BuddyPress **Installation Wizard** (or **Update Wizard** from within a multisite network), click on **BuddyPress** in the WordPress left sidebar.

The **BuddyPress Setup** involves five steps: **Components**, **Pages**, **Permalinks**, **Theme**, and **Finish**.

Components

The first step is to select the BuddyPress components we wish to enable for our site. The **Components** screen allows us to pick and choose the available BuddyPress features such as profiles, activity streams, groups, and forums.

By default the standard BuddyPress components are enabled. To disable any component, uncheck the checkbox next to the component name. The only feature educators may wish to turn off is the **Private Messaging** component. With private messaging disabled, students will be unable to send non-public messages to one another. This will cause all student-to-student interactions to remain public, simplifying the instructor's job of moderating student comments.

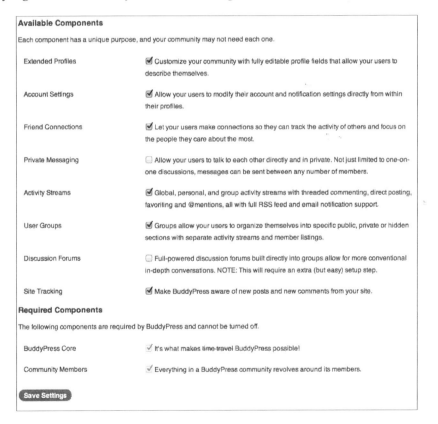

Once we have deselected any undesired components, click on the **Save & Next** button to proceed to the **Pages** option.

Pages

BuddyPress will automatically create new site pages for each of its features. The **Pages** screen allows us to select existing pages for this new content rather than creating a new page. This will not be necessary for most users. To proceed to the **Permalinks** screen, click on the **Save & Next** button.

Permalinks

BuddyPress requires **Permalinks**, such as those we enabled in *Chapter 1, Installing and Configuring WordPress*. If we are not already using permalinks we can change to a permalink URL structure now. Otherwise, we may click on the **Save & Next** button to proceed to **Theme** step of the installation.

Theme

BuddyPress requires specially formatted theme files to properly display the social content. Unfortunately, this means that many WordPress themes will not work with BuddyPress. From the **Theme** screen of the BuddyPress installation, choose to enable the default BuddyPress theme. With the default BuddyPress theme enabled, click on the **Save & Next** button to proceed to the final step of the activation process.

BuddyPress themes

We can later search for additional BuddyPress enabled themes. To do this visit the **Install Themes** screen of WordPress, check the **BuddyPress** checkbox under the **Features** heading, and click on the **Find Themes** button. This will present us with a list of available themes designed specifically for BuddyPress.

Finish

From the **Finish** screen we will receive the message that **The BuddyPress setup is complete, and your site is ready to go!** To complete the installation process and enable BuddyPress, click on the **Finish & Activate** button.

Registering student accounts

In order for students to utilize the social networking features of BuddyPress, they will need registered user accounts. If using a multisite network to create a network of student sites, our students will already have accounts and we may proceed past this step.

In the event that students need to be registered as new users, we may either individually add students ourselves or enable student self-registration.

Individually registering students

As the site administrator, we can add new student user accounts individually. While time consuming, this provides us with the greatest amount of control over the registration process.

To create a new user account:

1. Within WordPress, hover over **Users**, choose **Add New**.
2. In the **Add New User** portion of the screen, enter a username and an e-mail address.
3. Leave the user role as **Subscriber**. This will allow the student to interact with our site, but not make changes and edits to the site content.
4. Click on the **Add New User** button.
5. Repeat these steps for each student account needed.

Enabling student self-registration

As you can imagine, individually registering student accounts can be quite an arduous task. An efficient way of creating accounts is to temporarily enable new user self-registration. This will provide students with a brief window of opportunity to create accounts themselves. Once the time period has elapsed, we can disable new account creation to prevent non-students from registering.

To enable student self-registration:

1. Access the WordPress **General Settings** page by hovering over **Settings** in the WordPress sidebar and choosing **General**.

2. Check the **Anyone can register** box to allow new user registration.

3. Click on the **Save Changes** button.

4. Direct students to the registration page (http://example.org/register/) to complete the signup form.

Create an Account

Registering for this site is easy, just fill in the fields below and we'll get a new account set up for you in no time.

Account Details

Username (required)

Profile Details

Name (required)

Email Address (required)

Choose a Password (required)

Confirm Password (required)

Complete Sign Up

5. Once all students have registered, disable new user registration by returning to the WordPress **General Settings** screen, un-checking the **Anyone can register box** and clicking on the **Save Changes** button.

Activity

The activity stream of BuddyPress is the social hub of our site. When we install BuddyPress, a new page of our public site titled **Activity** is created. The **Activity** page acts in a similar fashion to the news feed of popular social networks. From the **Activity** page, registered site users are able to quickly share updates, comments, and links. This is an incredibly frictionless way for both instructors and students to post content to the class site.

One way in which I have seen the effectiveness of the BuddyPress activity stream is to encourage students to use it to post questions. On many occasions other students will respond to the question before the instructor has even had the opportunity to respond.

Using mentions, we can target replies and comments at specific students and encourage students to respond directly to one another. To mention another BuddyPress user, we simply add @username (with username replaced by the actual username) to an activity post.

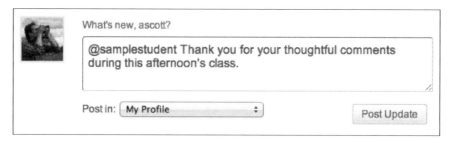

Whenever a user is mentioned, they will be notified through the **Mentions** tab of the **Activity** page. **Mentions** are helpful in encouraging student discussion as well as providing a simple means for instructors to direct information to a specific student.

Friend connections

Working in a similar fashion to popular social networks, BuddyPress allows users to request friend connections with one another. Friend connections allow users to see a stream of updates posted only by friends. The usefulness of friends in an education setting will come into play when forming **Groups** as discussed later in the chapter. For this reason, I advise adding each student as a friend within your BuddyPress site.

To add a friend, visit the **Members** page of the public WordPress site and click on the **Add Friend** button to the right of each member's name. This will send a friend request to each student or site user, which they must confirm.

When a student or user has a pending friend request, they will be notified by the **Notifications** in the site toolbar located at the top the screen. For students to approve friend requests, prompt them to log in to their account and visit the **Friends** page. The **Friends** page can be accessed by selecting **My Account** | **Friends** | **Requests** from the toolbar.

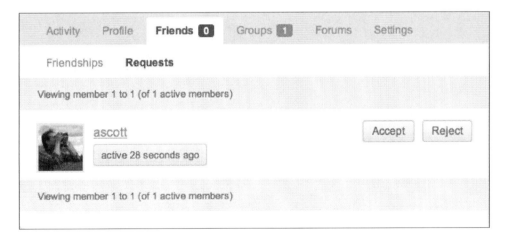

Groups

One of the killer features of BuddyPress is the ability to create **Groups**. Each **Group** has its own activity stream, allowing a subset of site users to communicate and collaborate. Only individuals enrolled in the group will be able to see and post to this activity stream. Groups are useful for separating the subsections of a course or to allow students to collaborate on a project.

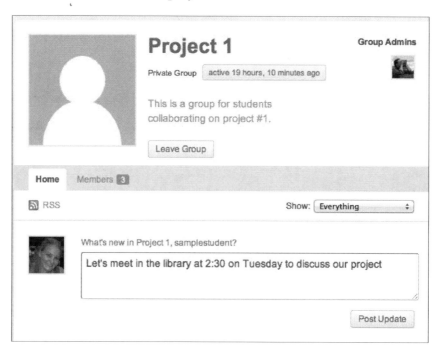

To create a group:

1. Visit the **Groups** page of our course website and click the **Create a Group** button.

2. We will then be taken to the **Details** screen where we are prompted to name the group and provide a brief description. Clearly labeling and describing the groups will prevent students from requesting access to an incorrect group.

3. The next step is to select an appropriate privacy option for the group. Choosing to set a group as **Private** will prevent non-group members from seeing the interactions of the group. From this screen we may also select who has the ability to add new members to a group. If we wish to retain control over the members of a group, set the **Group Invitations** option to **Group admins and mods only**.

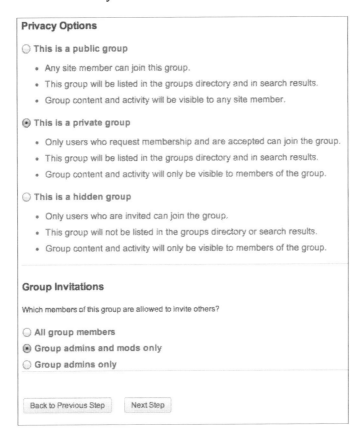

4. The **Avatar** screen allows us to select an image to represent the group. This is not necessary, but can be an easy way to differentiate groups.

5. The **Invites** screen allows us to select site users from our friend list to be added to the group. Select the appropriate students and click on the **Finish** button.

 Please note that if you wish to use group forums you should activate the forum option, as described in the following section, before creating the group.

Forums

Forums are an effective way of coordinating student discussion. Forums serve a different purpose than site **Activity**, as forums allow users to create and respond to posts within a given topic. BuddyPress does not enable forums by default, but allows us to create both a general forum for all site users as well as group specific forums.

To install a forum, visit the WordPress dashboard, hover over **BuddyPress** in the left sidebar and choose **Forums**. From the **Forums** screen we are able to install both **Forums for Groups** and **Site Wide Forums** by clicking the blue **Install Group Forums** or **Install Site Wide Forums** button.

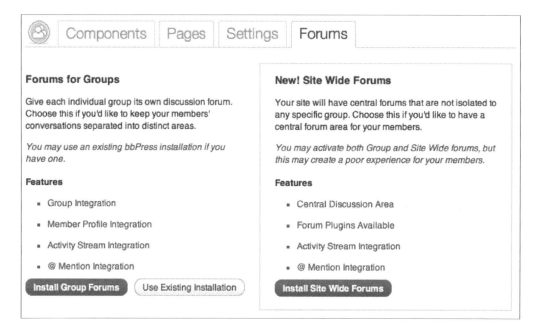

While it is possible to enable group and sitewide forums simultaneously, the distinction to site users is not clear, causing the experience for students to be confusing. I would recommend selecting only the type of forum that best meets your needs rather than installing both.

Group forums

Group forums will give the members of a group access to a separate discussion forum. Only group members will have access to post to a group forum. Forums can be useful when groups of students are coordinating information, such as a research project, which could otherwise be lost in a frequently updated activity stream.

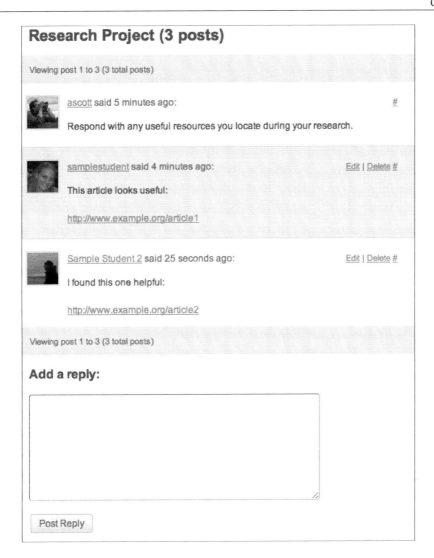

Research Project (3 posts)

Viewing post 1 to 3 (3 total posts)

ascott said 5 minutes ago: #

Respond with any useful resources you locate during your research.

samplestudent said 4 minutes ago: Edit | Delete #

This article looks useful:

http://www.example.org/article1

Sample Student 2 said 25 seconds ago: Edit | Delete #

I found this one helpful:

http://www.example.org/article2

Viewing post 1 to 3 (3 total posts)

Add a reply:

Post Reply

Sitewide forums

Sitewide forums provide a discussion forum that can be accessed by all registered site users. This can be a useful way for instructors to curate a discussion based on a particular topic or to encourage student collaboration.

Protecting student privacy

The **Private BuddyPress** plugin allows us to hide portions of our site from non-registered users, protecting the privacy of our students. To use the **Private BuddyPress** plugin, search for and activate the plugin from within WordPress.

Once the plugin is activated, the entire site will be blocked from non-registered users. We have the ability to change this to allow site visitors access to only the non-BuddyPress portions of the site.

To block the BuddyPress portion of the site for non-registered visitors, log in to the WordPress dashboard, hover over **Settings** in the left sidebar, and select **Privacy**.

From the **Privacy Settings** screen, check the boxes to exclude **Front page** and **Blog pages** from protection.

With these settings enabled, site visitors will be prompted to log in if they attempt to visit any BuddyPress area of the site such as **Activity**, **Users**, or **Groups**. Other areas of the site such as the home page and blog posts will remain public and accessible to all site visitors.

Summary

In this chapter, we've looked at how to create a small social network with the BuddyPress plugin. We discussed how to install and activate the BuddyPress plugin, and we explored student accounts, the activity page, friend connections, groups, forums, and student privacy.

In the next chapter we will install the BuddyPress Open Courseware plugin to turn our WordPress site into an effective course management system.

6

BuddyPress Courseware

The **BuddyPress (BP) Courseware** plugin by ScholarPress transforms our WordPress site into a learning management system. This plugin provides educators with the ability to post and organize course content, assignments, bibliographies, and schedules. BP Courseware works by extending the BuddyPress group functionality. Each courseware-enabled group receives a courseware dashboard where teachers and students can quickly access and post course content. The BP Courseware plugin is ideal for managing multiple courses by the same instructor or for an entire academic department.

In this chapter we'll cover how to install and configure the BP Courseware plugin. Once the plugin is installed, we'll develop content for a sample courseware course by adding course information, posting assignments, grading student assignments, creating a bibliography, and managing the course calendar.

Installing and configuring BP Courseware

As BP Courseware is a plugin that runs atop BuddyPress, we must have already installed, activated, and configured BuddyPress as described in *Chapter 5, Creating a Social Network with BuddyPress*.

To install BP Courseware, log in to the WordPress dashboard, hover over **Plugins** in the left sidebar, and choose **Add New**. Search for BuddyPress ScholarPress Courseware and install the plugin as described in *Chapter 3, Enhancing WordPress with Plugins*.

BuddyPress Courseware requires the **Private Messaging** BuddyPress component to be enabled. If you have disabled **Private Messaging**, as described in *Chapter 5, Creating a Social Network with BuddyPress*, you will be prompted to enable it before activating BuddyPress Courseware. To enable **Private Messaging**, log in to the WordPress dashboard and visit the BuddyPress **Components** screen.

BuddyPress Courseware settings

While BuddyPress Courseware will work immediately, there are a number of settings that can be adjusted to ensure that the plugin meets our needs. To access the BuddyPress Courseware settings, log in to the WordPress dashboard, hover over **BuddyPress** in the left sidebar, and select **Courseware**.

Global settings

BP Courseware integrates with BuddyPress groups for course management. By default, we must enable courseware individually for each group. Checking the **Enable Courseware globally** checkbox will turn courseware on for all new groups. This is useful if groups are used exclusively for course management.

If you intend to use BuddyPress groups for other purposes, such as student project collaboration, the **Enable Courseware globally** option should remain unchecked. In this scenario each group will require enabling courseware manually. To do so, follow the instructions given in the *Enabling BP Courseware* section later in the chapter.

Collaboration settings

Within BP Courseware we are able to define users as either teachers or students. By enabling the **Collaboration settings** option, any site user with a teacher role has the ability to edit and add courses, assignments, and schedules.

Make assignment responses private

When students submit an assignment their response is public to all site users. By enabling the **Make assignment responses private** feature, student responses will be visible only to the teachers and the student who has completed the assignment.

Gradebook default grade format

The default BuddyPress Courseware **Gradebook** format is numeric. Within the **Gradebook default grade format** settings we are able to choose between numeric, letter, or percentage grading for assignments.

Webservices API integration

BP Courseware has the ability to integrate with **WorldCat** and **ISBNdb** web services to aid in locating books and articles. To integrate these services with BuddyPress Courseware, follow the links from the BudddyPress Courseware settings screen to sign up for a free **API key**.

Customization

Cascading stylesheets (CSS) are the files that control the look and formatting of a web page. BuddyPress Courseware allows administrators with advanced web skills to create a custom stylesheet for fine grain control over the look of Courseware.

Renaming the groups page

BP Courseware utilizes the BuddyPress group feature for course content. While the term **Groups** makes sense in the context of a standard BuddyPress installation, it can be confusing when using BuddyPress Courseware as a learning management system. To prevent this confusion, I find it helpful to rename the **Groups** page to **Courses**.

To rename **Groups**:

1. Log in to the WordPress dashboard.
2. Create a new WordPress page titled **Courses** by hovering over **Pages** in the left sidebar, and choosing **Add New**. Title the page **Courses**, leaving the page content blank, and click on the blue **Publish** button.
3. Adjust the BuddyPress page settings by hovering over **BuddyPress** in the left sidebar and selecting the **Pages** tab. In the menu next to **User Groups**, select the **Courses** option and click on the **Save** button.

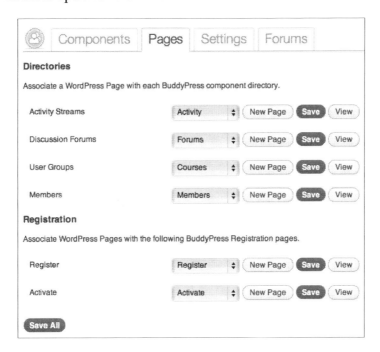

4. Delete the **Groups** page by clicking on **Pages** in the left sidebar. From the **All Pages** screen, hover over the **Groups** page and click on the red **Trash** link.

Setting Courses as the site home page

In *Chapter 2, Setting up our Class Site*, we created a page titled **Home** and set it as the static front page of our WordPress site. Using the BuddyPress Courseware plugin, we may wish to enable our **Courses** page as the site's front page. Doing so will allow students to quickly access course information and prevent confusion regarding how to find the courseware dashboard.

To enable the **Courses** page as our site's home page:

1. Log in to the WordPress dashboard.
2. If you have not already done so, create an empty page titled Blog, as described in *Chapter 2, Setting up our Class Site*.
3. Hover over **Settings** in the left sidebar and select the **Reading** tab.
4. From the **Reading Settings** screen, select **Front page displays | A static page** option.
5. Select **Courses** from the **Front page** menu choices and **Blog** as the **Posts page**.

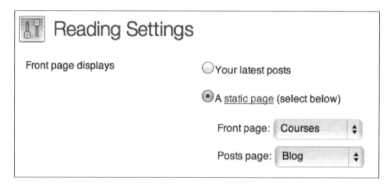

Creating a course

When setting up a course we must first create a BuddyPress group, as described in *Chapter 5, Creating a Social Network with BuddyPress*.

To create course or group:

1. From our public facing site, visit the **Courses** page (or **Groups** if not renamed).

2. Click on the **Create a Group** button.

3. From the **Details** screen, provide a **Group Name** such as the course name and section number and enter a **Group Description** such as the course catalog information.

4. On the **Privacy Options** page, select **This is a public group**, allowing any site member to join.

5. Complete the installation by optionally adding an avatar image and inviting members, as described in *Chapter 5, Creating a Social Network with BuddyPress*.

Enabling BP Courseware

Once the course group has been created, we may enable BP Courseware. This step may be skipped, if we selected **Enable Courseware globally** from the **BuddyPress Courseware** settings screen.

To enable BP Courseware:

1. Visit the page of the newly created group.

2. Click on the **Admin** tab.

3. Click on the **Courseware** link from the row of links below the **Admin** tab.

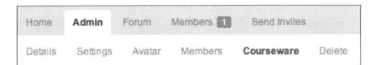

4. Below **Courseware Status**, select **Enable** to enable BP Courseware for the group. Optionally, if you wish to keep student assignment responses private, select **Enable** below **Private Responses**.

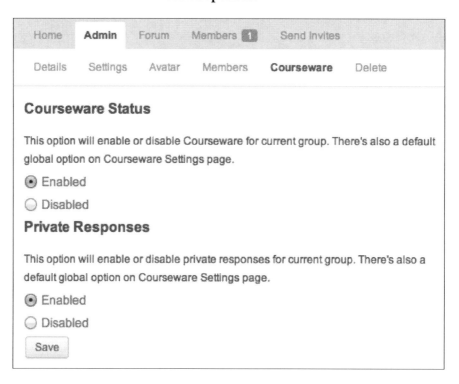

5. Click on the **Save** button.

Courseware dashboard

Within BP Courseware, the courseware dashboard acts as the course home screen for both instructors and students. From the courseware dashboard, instructors are able to add and manage course content. Students use the dashboard to access course materials and submit assignments. To access the courseware dashboard, visit the **Courses** page (or **Groups** if unchanged) and click on the **Courseware** link located below the course/group description.

The teacher dashboard appears as shown in the following screenshot:

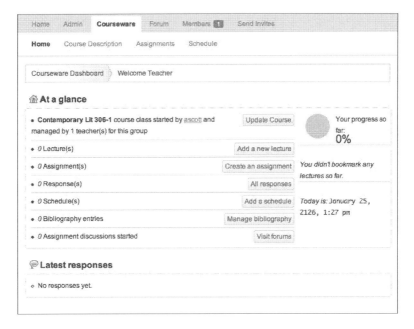

The student dashboard appears as shown in the following screenshot:

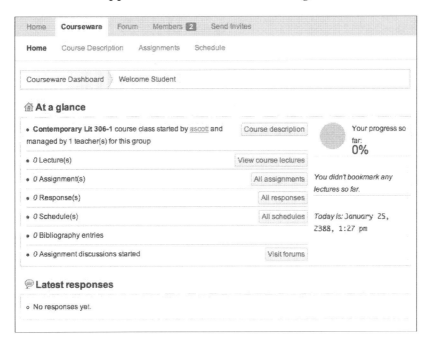

Adding course content

Adding course content to BP Courseware allows educators to easily organize and share course information with students. The BP Courseware plugin provides a structure for managing course lectures, assignments, quizzes, grades, resources, and schedules.

Lectures

Adding lecture information allows instructors to share course notes, resources, and slides with students in a structured format. While the term lecture implies the lecture format of university courses, I find it useful to think of *lectures* in terms of teaching units. The lecture pages can serve as a resource for a chunk of course content.

To add a new lecture, click on the **Add a new lecture** button from the course dashboard. We may then edit the content of the lecture much in the same way as a WordPress post adding text, images, links, and embedded media.

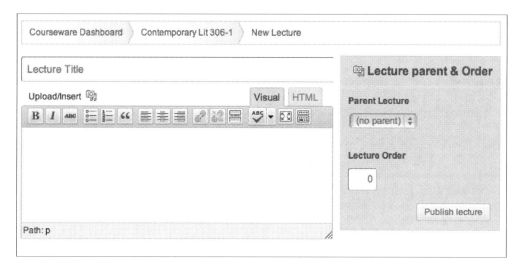

Lectures will appear in the **Latest Lectures** section of course dashboard, with the most recently posted lecture appearing at the top. This allows students to quickly access the most recently posted course lecture.

Assignments

BP Courseware provides a means for us to post assignments and collect student responses. The assignments can take multiple formats, allowing students to respond to questions, upload a file, or embed media.

Posting assignments as a teacher

As a teacher, we have the ability to post assignments. To post an assignment, visit the course dashboard and click on the **Create an assignment** button. This will take us to the **New Assignment** screen. From the **New Assignment** screen, we may enter the details of the assignment.

From the **New Assignment** screen, assign a title to the assignment and enter the assignment description and necessary information. This acts much in the same way as WordPress posts, allowing us to enter text, images, media, and links.

In the right column, we may choose the corresponding lecture topic and select the assignment due date.

Once the assignment information is complete, click on the **Publish assignment** button to make it visible to students.

Submitting assignments as a student

Students can access assignments by clicking on the **All Assignments** button or viewing the **Latest Assignments** from the course dashboard. By clicking on the **Assignment Title**, students can see the detailed assignment information written by the instructor. Clicking on the **Add a response** button, will give the students an opportunity to submit the assignment.

For standard assignments, students will be presented with a text input area similar to the WordPress post editor. Within this text area, students may type a written response, add links, embed media, and attach files.

Viewing student responses

Instructors have access to all student assignment responses, while students are only able to view their own. To view student assignment responses, visit the **individual assignment** page and click on the **Responses** button, located in the right sidebar. This will present us with a list of student responses. Clicking on the **individual assignment** link, will take us to a screen containing the student's assignment response.

Gradebook

BP Courseware provides us with a **Gradebook** feature for assessing student assignments. To access the Gradebook, visit an individual assignment page and click on the **Gradebook** button, located in the right sidebar. This will take us to the **Gradebook** screen for the assignment.

For each student, we are given the option to enter a grade value, a private comment, and a public comment. Once the grades and comments have been entered, we may click on the **Save grades** button.

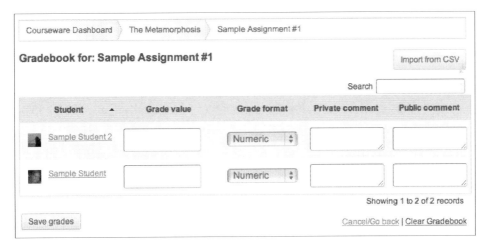

After an assignment has been graded, students will receive a message containing the grade. Students will be alerted to this message by a notification, but may access their grades directly by visiting the individual assignment page. The grade is posted in the **Assignment Meta** sidebar of the **assignment** page.

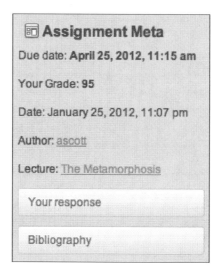

Bibliography

The **Bibliography** is designed so that educators can easily maintain a list of course materials and resources. To add entries to the bibliography, visit the **Courseware** dashboard and click on the **Manage bibliography** button. From the **Bibliography** page we may add entries manually or import them by pasting information from BibTeX. The bibliography is ideal for courses utilizing a wide range of materials.

 BibTeX is a tool for formatting references. It is typically used in conjunction with the **LaTeX** typesetting system. More information can be found at http://www.bibtex.org.

Schedule and calendar

The BuddyPress **Schedule** page functions as a course calendar, automatically containing assignment due dates as well as manually managed schedule items. To view the course calendar, visit the **Courseware** dashboard and click on the **Schedules** link.

To schedule more items, click on the **Add a schedule** button from the **Courseware** dashboard. Complete the **New Schedule** form and click on the **Publish Schedule** button once it is complete. New schedule items will be added to the calendar as well as featured in a list format on the **Schedules** page.

Teacher and student roles

There are two roles within BP Courseware: student and teacher. By default, the site admin has a teacher role and all additional site users are considered students. Users may request teacher role permissions by adjusting the BuddyPress account settings.

To request teacher privileges:

1.   Prompt the user to log in to BuddyPress.
2.   Once logged in the user will access the **Edit Profile** screen by hovering over **My Account** in the BuddyPress toolbar and selecting **Profile | Edit**.

3. From the edit profile screen, the user will need to click on the **Courseware** button.

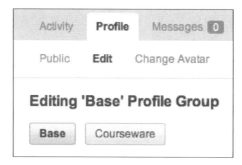

4. The user may then select the **Apply for Teacher** radio button and click on the **Save Changes** button.

Prior to being granted access as a teacher, the site admin will be required to approve the user's request. The site admin will receive a message stating that the user has requested teacher access.

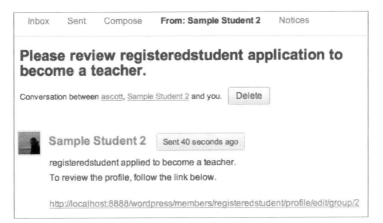

To approve the access, click on the link contained in the message to visit the user's profile screen and select the **Teacher** role.

Help and support

The BP Courseware plugin is in active development and evolving to meet the needs of a diverse set of educators. ScholarPress, the group behind the BP Courseware plugin, provides a number of resources including a BuddyPress Courseware Handbook (`http://coursewa.re/handbook`), **user support forums** (`http://buddypress.org/community/groups/buddypress-courseware/forum/`), and a list of recommended additional plugins. We can access this information through the **Help** button located at the top of the **BuddyPress Courseware** settings screen on the WordPress dashboard. For the latest BP Courseware updates and project news, visit the ScholarPress BuddyPress Courseware site (`http://coursewa.re`).

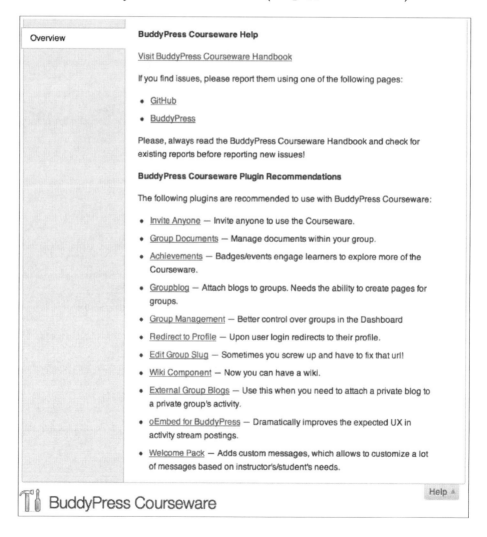

Summary

In this chapter we saw how the BuddyPress Courseware plugin can turn WordPress into a fully-featured learning management system. To accomplish this, we installed the BP Courseware plugin, added course content, created course assignments, managed the course bibliography, and maintained the course schedule.

In the next, and final chapter, we will look at how we can update, maintain, and secure our WordPress installation.

7
Site Management

Throughout the book we've explored the possibilities of using WordPress in an education setting. Self hosting a content management system, such as WordPress, requires administrators to perform regular site management. In this chapter we'll walk through the processes of backing up our database, improving site performance, securing our WordPress installation, and keeping WordPress up-to-date. Performing proper site management will ensure that our students have a seamless experience using our site.

Site backups

WordPress stores our site's content within a database. Backing up our database will prevent the loss of pages, posts, and comments in the event of a database error.

While our database can be backed up manually, it should not surprise you to learn that there are many plugins that will automate the process. The WordPress Database Backup plugin by Austin Matzko (`http://wordpress.org/extend/plugins/wp-db-backup/`) will allow us to not only download database backups, but will also e-mail them to us on a regular basis, creating a simple and automatic backup solution.

To install the WordPress Database Backup plugin, search for **WP-DB-Backup** from the **Install Plugins** WordPress screen.

Once the plugin is installed and activated, visit the **Backup** screen by hovering over **Tools** in the WordPress left sidebar and selecting **Backup**.

To perform a manual backup, scroll to the **Backup Options** link and click on the **Backup now!** button. This will download a database backup to your computer.

Regularly e-mailed database backups can be scheduled within the **Scheduled Backup** settings. Select the frequency of the desired backups and click on the **schedule backup** button. For most sites, I choose to back up on a weekly basis, ensuring that I will never lose more than a week's content.

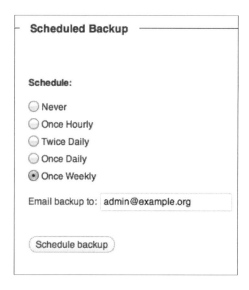

While **WP-DB-Backup** creates a copy of our site's database, it does not back up the entire site. Uploaded files such as documents, images, plugins, and theme files are not contained within the database. For backing up these files, I recommend using the **Backuper** plugin (`http://wordpress.org/extend/plugins/backuper/`). Similar to **WP-DB-Backup**, Backuper will send scheduled e-mails containing a site backup.

This backup includes both the database files as well as uploads, plugins, and themes. I do not recommend using only the Backuper plugin, as the size of the site's files can at times cause the e-mail backups to fail. However, this plugin remains a simple and effective way to create a full site backup.

To install the Backuper plugin, search for **Backuper** from the **Install Plugins** WordPress screen. At the time of writing, the Backuper plugin appears under its former name, **WordPress Backup**.

Once the plugin is installed and activated, visit the **Backup** screen by hovering over **Settings** in the WordPress left sidebar and select the **Backuper** plugin.

From the Backuper screen, select the **Everything/Full-backup** checkbox, select the frequency of backups, and enter the e-mail address to receive the backups.

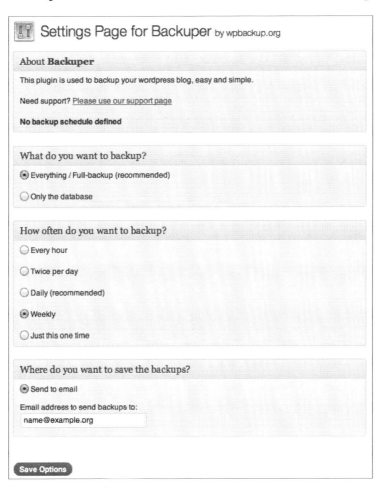

Site performance

A slow website creates a frustrating experience for students. By optimizing our site performance, site visitors will be able to access course information more quickly.

The first step to site optimization is to disable any unused plugins. Throughout the book, I have recommended dozens of plugins that will enhance a WordPress site for education, but running too many active plugins can significantly decrease site performance. Once you have found the right plugin configuration for your site, be sure to disable and delete the plugins that are unused.

WP Super Cache

WP Super Cache is a caching plugin that will dramatically improve the speed of our site. Caching creates static files of our posts and pages, which load much more quickly than the dynamic WordPress files. One of the reasons I like WP Super Cache is that it provides a simple setup while retaining advanced options for experienced users.

To use WP Super Cache, install and activate the WP Super Cache plugin. Once the plugin is activated, visit the **WP Super Cache Settings** screen by hovering over **Settings** in the WordPress left sidebar and choosing **WP Super Cache**. To enable caching, simply select the **Caching On** radio button and click on the **Update Status** button.

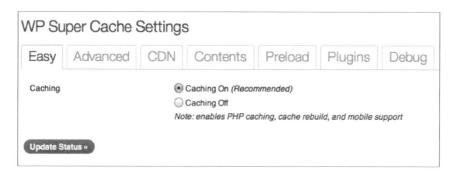

Better WP Minify

Better WP Minify is another useful plugin for speeding up WordPress. Better WP Minify works by reducing the size of the HTML, CSS, and JavaScript files. While the speed enhancement will not be as dramatic as with WP Super Cache, using Better WP Minify in conjunction with WP Super Cache will aid in improving site load times. To use Better WP Minify, simply install and activate the Better WP Minify plugin (`http://wordpress.org/extend/plugins/bwp-minify/`).

Site security

The popularity of the WordPress platform has led to attempts by hackers to exploit WordPress security vulnerabilities. While the instances of hacked WordPress installations which are up-to-date is uncommon, it is important to take preventative security measures.

The most important security precaution we can take is to make sure our WordPress installation is kept up-to-date. The WordPress team works to quickly patch security vulnerabilities. Whenever an update is available, we are notified through the WordPress dashboard. Follow the update process as described later in the chapter to ensure your WordPress installation is updated and secure.

Secure WordPress

Secure WordPress is a plugin that will automatically make a number of security tweaks to our WordPress installation. To use Secure WordPress, simply install and activate the plugin. The plugin works by automatically removing some of the WordPress security vulnerabilities that could be exploited by hackers, such as the WordPress version number, login page error information, and unnecessary information for non-admin users.

WP Security Scan

The **WP Security Scan** plugin, scans our WordPress installation for security vulnerabilities and provides information on how to resolve the issue. Once the WP Security Scan plugin is installed and activated, click on the **WSD Security** link in the WordPress left sidebar.

The **WP-Security Admin tools** screen will display a list of potential security vulnerabilities and offer recommended solutions.

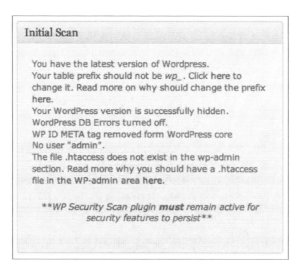

Updating WordPress

The WordPress team regularly releases updates to the WordPress software. These updates contain bug fixes, improvements, security patches, and additional features. It is a good idea to make sure that you are always running the latest version of WordPress.

 Before updating WordPress, it is recommended that the user backs up the database as described earlier in the chapter.

When a WordPress update is available, an update notice will appear at the top of all WordPress dashboard screens as shown in the following screenshot:

WordPress 3.3.1 is available! Please update now.

To update WordPress, click on the **Update Now** link in the notification or hover over **Dashboard** in the WordPress left sidebar and select **Updates**. Clicking on the **Update Now** button will download and install the latest version of WordPress.

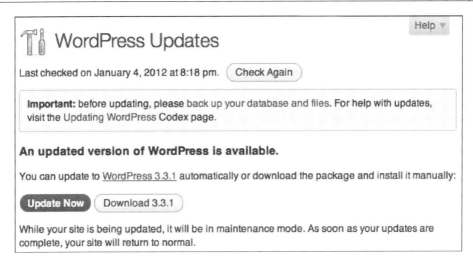

Summary

In this chapter we learned to manage our WordPress installation through backups, site performance, security, and updates. By using an automated backup tool, we can ensure that our database is regularly backed up. Caching and minifying plugins improve site performance. Security plugins will scan and enhance the security of WordPress. Most importantly, keeping WordPress up-to-date will increase both the security and functionality of our site.

WordPress Resources and Plugins

Throughout the book I have attempted to provide you with the examples, resources, and plugins I have found most helpful when using WordPress in an education environment. In this chapter I will point you to additional resources and provide a directory of the plugins mentioned in the book.

WordPress resources

There are a handful of sites I turn to when seeking WordPress guidance. These sites are incredibly useful for solving WordPress issues, finding plugins, and seeing site examples.

WordPress Codex

The WordPress Codex (`http://codex.wordpress.org`) serves as the "online manual" for WordPress, which continues to evolve and expand with the platform. The Codex is full of resources for both users and developers seeking to extend WordPress.

WordPress Support Forum

The WordPress Support Forum (`http://wordpress.org/support/`) is an effective way to learn from the large WordPress community. In the forums, users request assistance both regarding the WordPress core and specific plugin help.

WordPress Showcase: Education

The Education category of the WordPress Showcase (`http://wordpress.org/showcase/tag/education/`) serves as a gallery of education related to WordPress sites. This is a great way to get inspiration and see how others are utilizing WordPress in an education setting.

wp-edu discussion list

The wp-edu discussion list (`http://lists.automattic.com/mailman/listinfo/wp-edu`) is a low volume e-mail discussion list. The list serves as a place to request and discuss practical WordPress advice that is unique to an education setting.

Digging into WordPress

Digging into WordPress (`http://digwp.com`) is a fantastic all-purpose site and book by Chris Coyier and Jeff Star. I hold the advice given by Chris and Jeff in high regard, particularly when it comes to issues such as security and backups.

Plugin directory

Plugin name	Plugin website
Add Multiple Users to WordPress	`http://www.happynuclear.com/sandbox/amu/add-multiple-users-for-wordpress.php`
Akismet	`http://wordpress.org/extend/plugins/akismet/`
Anthologize	`http://anthologize.org/`
bbPress	`http://bbpress.org/`
BuddyPress	`http://buddypress.org/`
Calendar	`http://wordpress.org/extend/plugins/calendar/`
Contact Form 7	`http://contactform7.com`
Diamond Multisite Widgets	`http://wordpress.org/extend/plugins/diamond-multisite-widgets/`
Disqus	`http://disqus.com/`
Enable Multi-Site	`http://wordpress.org/extend/plugins/wordpress-multi-site-enabler-plugin-v10/`
Grader	`http://wordpress.org/extend/plugins/grader/`
Intense Debate Comments	`http://wordpress.org/extend/plugins/intensedebate/`

Plugin name	Plugin website
Jetpack	http://jetpack.me/
Multisite Plugin Manager	http://wordpress.org/extend/plugins/multisite-plugin-manager/
Multisite Recent Posts Widget	http://wordpress.org/extend/plugins/multisite-recent-posts-widget/
New Blog Templates	http://premium.wpmudev.org/project/new-blog-template
ScholarPress BuddyPress Courseware	http://coursewa.re/
ScholarPress Courseware	http://scholarpress.net/courseware/
Secure WordPress	http://wordpress.org/extend/plugins/secure-wordpress/
Semi-Private Comments	http://wordpress.org/extend/plugins/semi-private-comments/
Simple Facebook Connect	http://wordpress.org/extend/plugins/simple-facebook-connect/
ThreeWP Activity Monitor	http://wordpress.org/extend/plugins/threewp-activity-monitor/
WordPress Database Backup	http://wordpress.org/extend/plugins/wp-db-backup/
Better WP Minify	http://wordpress.org/extend/plugins/bwp-minify/
WordPress Mobile Pack	http://wordpress.org/extend/plugins/wordpress-mobile-pack/
WP Security Scan	http://wordpress.org/extend/plugins/wp-security-scan/
WP Super Cache	http://ocaoimh.ie/wp-super-cache/
WP Survey and Quiz Tool	http://wordpress.org/extend/plugins/wp-survey-and-quiz-tool/
WP to Twitter	http://wordpress.org/extend/plugins/wp-to-twitter/

Index

Q

QuickPress option 16
Quiz Tool plugin 54, 55

R

reading settings 21
resources, WordPress
  WordPress Codex 121
  WordPress showcase 122
  WordPress Support Forum 121
  wp-edu discussion list 122
RSS 21

S

Save Draft button 27
Save grades button 105
Save Menu button 45
schedule backup button 114
ScholarPress BuddyPress Courseware
  about 123
  site 110
ScholarPress Courseware plugin 52, 53, 123
Secure WordPress plugin 117, 123
Semi-Private Comments plugin 58, 123
settings, WordPress
  discussion settings 22
  general settings 20
  media settings 22
  permalinks 22
  privacy settings 22
  reading settings 21
  writing settings 20, 21
Simple Facebook Connect 123
Simple Facebook Connect plugin 60
Site Address 72
site backups 113
site management
  about 113
  backups 113, 114
  performance 116
  security 117
site performance
  about 116

Better WP Minify plugin, using 117
  WP Super Cache 116
site security
  about 117
  Secure WordPress plugin 117
  WP Security Scan plugin 117
Site Title 72
Slug 37
social plugin
  about 60
  Simple Facebook Connect 60
  WP to Twitter 60
student 107
student accounts registration
  about 85
  new user account, creating 85
  self registration, enabling 86
student privacy
  protecting 94
syllabus page
  creating 30, 31

T

Tags box 33
teacher
  about 107
  privileges, requesting 107-109
theme installation
  about 73
  Network Enabled themes 73
themes
  about 39
  adding 40
  Manage Themes screen 40
  new themes, searching 40
ThreeWP Activity Monitor 76, 123
Trash option 31

U

Unlink button 26
Update Now link 118
Update Plugins button 65
Update Status button 116
user support forums 110

V

view post link 18
Visual editor 25

W

widget
  about 41
  adding 41
  Categories 42
  Recent Posts 42
  Search 42
  Tag Cloud 42
  Text 42
WordPress
  about 82
  admin bar 15
  digging into 122
  Help link 16
  installing 7
  installing, with purchased hosting 9
  manual installation 11-15
  menu 43
  multisite feature 67
  overview 15, 16
  page, creating 17
  plugins 47
  post, creating 17
  QuickPress option 16
  resources 121
  settings 20
  site login 15
  themes 39
  updating 118
WordPress Codex 48, 69, 121
WordPress Database Backup 113, 123
WordPress Mobile Pack plugin 64, 123
WordPress Showcase 122
WordPress Support Forum 121
WorldCat 96
WP-DB-Backup, Backuper 114
wp-edu discussion list 122
WPMU DEV website 75
WP-Security Admin tools screen 118
WP Security Scan plugin 117, 123
WP Super Cache 116, 123
WP Survey and Quiz Tool 123
WP Survey plugin 54, 55
WP to Twitter plugin 60, 123

Thank you for buying
WordPress for Education

About Packt Publishing

Packt, pronounced 'packed', published its first book "*Mastering phpMyAdmin for Effective MySQL Management*" in April 2004 and subsequently continued to specialize in publishing highly focused books on specific technologies and solutions.

Our books and publications share the experiences of your fellow IT professionals in adapting and customizing today's systems, applications, and frameworks. Our solution based books give you the knowledge and power to customize the software and technologies you're using to get the job done. Packt books are more specific and less general than the IT books you have seen in the past. Our unique business model allows us to bring you more focused information, giving you more of what you need to know, and less of what you don't.

Packt is a modern, yet unique publishing company, which focuses on producing quality, cutting-edge books for communities of developers, administrators, and newbies alike. For more information, please visit our website: www.packtpub.com.

About Packt Open Source

In 2010, Packt launched two new brands, Packt Open Source and Packt Enterprise, in order to continue its focus on specialization. This book is part of the Packt Open Source brand, home to books published on software built around Open Source licences, and offering information to anybody from advanced developers to budding web designers. The Open Source brand also runs Packt's Open Source Royalty Scheme, by which Packt gives a royalty to each Open Source project about whose software a book is sold.

Writing for Packt

We welcome all inquiries from people who are interested in authoring. Book proposals should be sent to author@packtpub.com. If your book idea is still at an early stage and you would like to discuss it first before writing a formal book proposal, contact us; one of our commissioning editors will get in touch with you.

We're not just looking for published authors; if you have strong technical skills but no writing experience, our experienced editors can help you develop a writing career, or simply get some additional reward for your expertise.

WordPress 3 Cookbook

ISBN: 978-1-84951-460-6   Paperback: 328 pages

Over 100 recipes to help you enhance your
WordPress site!

1. Take your WordPress site to the next level with
   solutions to common WordPress problems that
   make your site better, smarter, faster, and more
   secure

2. Enhance your SEO and make more money
   online by applying simple hacks

3. Rich with screenshots and practical tasks that
   you will find quite useful

WordPress 3 Site Blueprints

ISBN: 978-1-847199-36-2   Paperback: 300 pages

Ready-made plans for 9 different professional
WordPress sites

1. Everything you need to build a varied
   collection of feature-rich customized WordPress
   websites for yourself

2. Transform a static website into a dynamic
   WordPress blog

3. In-depth coverage of several WordPress themes
   and plugins

4. Packed with screenshots and step-by-step
   instructions to help you complete each site

Please check **www.PacktPub.com** for information on our titles

WordPress Plugin Development: Beginner's Guide

ISBN: 978-1-847193-59-9   Paperback: 296 pages

Build powerful, interactive plugins for your blog and to share online

1. Everything you need to create and distribute your own plug-ins following WordPress coding standards

2. Walk through the development of six complete, feature-rich, real-world plug-ins that are being used by thousands of WP users

3. Written by Vladimir Prelovac, WordPress expert and developer of WordPress plug-ins such as Smart YouTube and Plugin Central

WordPress 3 Complete

ISBN: 978-1-84951-410-1   Paperback: 344 pages

Create your own complete website or blog from scratch with WordPress

1. Learn everything you need for creating your own feature-rich website or blog from scratch

2. Clear and practical explanations of all aspects of WordPress

3. In-depth coverage of installation, themes, plugins, and syndication

4. Explore WordPress as a fully functional content management system

Please check **www.PacktPub.com** for information on our titles

46174413R00081

Made in the USA
Lexington, KY
25 October 2015